Peter Kropotkin

ANARCHISM & ANARCHIST COMMUNISM

Edited by Nicolas Walter

FREEDOM PRESS
LONDON
1993

Published by Freedom Press
84B Whitechapel High Street
London E1 7QX

Anarchism first published in 1910
Anarchist Communism first published in 1887
This edition first published in 1987
Reprinted 1993
Editorial material © Freedom Press and Nicolas Walter 1987
ISBN 0 900384 34 4

Freedom Press, founded in 1886, are the publishers of the fortnightly journal *Freedom* and the quarterly magazine *The Raven*, as well as of a long and growing list of anarchist books and pamphlets. Please send for our latest catalogue.

This pamphlet has been produced with the help of Heiner Becker, Christine Morris, Vernon Richards, Carol Saunders, Rufus Segar, and the Friends of Freedom Press.

Printed and typeset by Aldgate Press
84B Whitechapel High Street
London E1 7QX

INTRODUCTION

PETER KROPOTKIN was born in 1842 into the aristocracy of Tsarist Russia, was educated at an élite military school, and served as an army officer; but he became a Populist, and resigned his commission in 1867. He was soon well known as an explorer and geographer; but he became a socialist, and then an anarchist in 1872. He took an active part in the revolutionary movement, was arrested in 1874, but escaped in 1876, and lived in Western Europe until 1917. He returned to Russia during the Revolution, and died there in 1921.

During his first decade in the West, in the late 1870s and early 1880s, Kropotkin became the leading propagandist in the international anarchist movement. He adopted the new theory of anarchist communism, which combined the best of radical liberalism and revolutionary socialism in one economic, social and political system; and he attempted to base anarchism on natural science, especially on biological evolution. After being expelled from Switzerland in 1881 and imprisoned in France from 1883 to 1886, he settled in England, where he lived as an honoured exile for more than thirty years.

During this period he earned his living as a writer, specialising in scientific journalism. At the same time he produced a great deal of political journalism, which generally took two forms — anarchist articles in the anarchist press, especially the French paper which he helped to found in Geneva in 1879 as *Le Révolté*, which continued in Paris as *La Révolte* and then as *Les Temps Nouveaux* until 1914, and the English paper which he helped to found in London in 1886 as *Freedom*, which continued on and off under various names for more than a century, and still appears; and more general articles in the liberal press, especially weekly and monthly periodicals and reference books. Most of his books consisted of collections of some of these articles — the anarchist articles appearing as *Words of a Rebel* (1885), *The Conquest of Bread* (1892), *Modern Science and Anarchism* (1901-1913), and *Act for Yourselves* (1987), and the more general articles appearing as *In Russian and French Prisons* (1887), *Fields, Factories and Workshops* (1899), *Memoirs of a Revolutionist* (1899), *Mutual Aid* (1902), and *Ethics* (1922).

However, he was occasionally able to contribute explicitly anarchist material to non-anarchist publications, and two of the most important such items are reprinted together here.

Anarchist Communism first appeared in 1887 as a pair of articles in *The Nineteenth Century*, the leading monthly paper which was founded in 1877 by James Knowles, the greatest editor of the age, and which was an influential voice of the liberal intelligentsia and indeed of the Liberal Establishment. Kropotkin was a frequent contributor from 1883 until 1919, generally on scientific but occasionally on political subjects, and was a personal friend of Knowles from 1886 until his death in 1908. It has been suggested that Kropotkin was out of place in this company. But the contributors to *The Nineteenth Century* included not only such leaders of culture and society as Gladstone and Chamberlain, Tennyson and Arnold, Spencer and Huxley, Swinburne and Wilde, but also such representatives of radical causes as John Ruskin and William Morris, Frederic Harrison and W. K. Clifford, Auberon Herbert and Henry George, G. J. Holyoake and H. M. Hyndman, Millicent Fawcett and Beatrice Webb, Annie Besant and L. S. Bevington, John Burns and Tom Mann, and Kropotkin properly belonged among the latter as the authoritative exponent of mainstream anarchism; and extracts from these two articles were appropriately included in Michael Goodwin's anthology from the paper, *Nineteenth-Century Opinion* (1951).

The titles of the two articles were significant — 'The Scientific Bases of Anarchy' (February 1887) would remind readers of the positivist tradition of Saint-Simon and Comte, Spencer and Huxley (and perhaps of the still little-known Marx and Engels), which sought to base social and political ideology not on religious or philosophical speculation but on physical and natural science; and 'The Coming Anarchy' (August 1887) would remind readers of Herbert Spencer's 'The Coming Slavery', which appeared as an article in *The Contemporary Review* (April 1884) and then as a chapter in *The Man versus the State* (1884), and which criticised the parallel growth of state capitalism and state socialism.

This pair of articles was by no means Kropotkin's first or last or fullest summary of anarchist theory in general or of anarchist communism in particular. Indeed, at the time when they appeared, he was explaining his ideas in greater detail both in French in *La Révolte* (in the articles reprinted as *The Conquest of Bread*) and in English in *Freedom* (in the articles reprinted as *Act for Yourselves*), and also in many lectures and discussions. Nor was this the only defence of anarchism to appear in the liberal press; Spencer's articles in *The Contemporary Review* were accompanied by 'Anarchy: By an Anarchist' (May 1884), the anarchist being Kropotkin's comrade Elisée Reclus. But *Anarchist Communism* is distinguished by being particularly clear and straightforward.

Anarchism was written in 1905, and first appeared in 1910 as an article in the eleventh edition of the *Encyclopaedia Britannica*. This was first published in Scotland in 1768-1771 and was established as the best-known reference book in the English-speaking world. As a leading Russian geographer, Kropotkin contributed articles on Russian geography to the ninth, tenth and eleventh editions, which appeared between 1875 and 1911, and he was a personal friend of one of the editors, William Robertson Smith, from 1886 until his death in 1894. As the best-known anarchist in the world, who happened to be living in Britain, he was also invited to contribute the article on anarchism for the eleventh edition, which happened to be the last one published in Britain and which is still generally considered to be the best edition of all.

This article was by no means Kropotkin's first or last or fullest summary of anarchist history. Before the *Encyclopaedia Britannica* article, he had already produced a historical study of anarchism from the point of view of natural and social science, which appeared as *Modern Science and Anarchism* first in Russian (in London in

1901 and in Moscow in 1906), in French and English (in 1903), and then in several other languages. And after the *Encyclopaedia Britannica* article, he produced an expanded version of it and of the sections of *Modern Science and Anarchism* describing the development of anarchism, which appeared in French and English (in 1911) and in Russian (in London in 1912); the whole revised work appeared as the English booklet *Modern Science and Anarchism* (published by the Freedom Press in 1912) and in a slightly longer form as the first part of the French book *La science moderne et l'anarchie* (1913), and then in several other languages. He also produced a more straightforward account of 'The Development of Anarchist Ideas', which appeared in the *Encyclopédie du mouvement syndicaliste* (1912) and was also translated into several other languages (though not English).

Kropotkin was much helped in all this historical work by his old friends James Guillaume and Varlaam Cherkezov, and especially by Max Nettlau, who became the first (and remains the finest) historian of anarchism and who provided most of the detailed information about anarchist individuals and publications.

Both *Anarchism* and *Anarchist Communism* were frequently reprinted and translated into other languages for half a century, and both are still well worth re-reading as respectively a clear summary of anarchist theory and a clear account of anarchist communism, written for non-anarchist readers. Nevertheless a qualification should be entered. Kropotkin was during his life, and still is long after his death, the best-known anarchist writer, and he was also one of the most attractive and impressive members of the anarchist movement. But he was never accepted as an authority, even by his closest associates, and although his work is always interesting and instructive, it is also open to plenty of criticism.

It is certainly easy enough to find fault both with his general assumptions and with some of his detailed points, but he was in many ways a pioneer, and his philosophical and historical ideas were and still are important to the anarchist ideology. And although much of his work has inevitably been superseded or contradicted, most of it remains as valid as or even more valid than before.

Nicolas Walter   February 1987

1

ANARCHISM

ANARCHISM (from the Greek *an-* and *archē*, contrary to authority), the name given to a principle or theory of life and conduct under which society is conceived without government — harmony in such a society being obtained, not by submission to law, or by obedience to any authority, but by free agreements concluded between the various groups, territorial and professional, freely constituted for the sake of production and consumption, as also for the satisfaction of the infinite variety of needs and aspirations of a civilised being. In a society developed on these lines, the voluntary associations which already now begin to cover all the fields of human activity would take a still greater extension so as to substitute themselves for the State in all its functions. They would represent an interwoven network, composed of an infinite variety of groups and federations of all sizes and degrees, local, regional, national and international — temporary or more or less permanent — for all possible purposes: production, consumption and exchange, communications, sanitary arrangements, education, mutual protection, defence of the territory, and so on; and, on the other side, for the satisfaction of an ever-increasing number of scientific, artistic, literary and sociable needs. Moreover, such a society would represent nothing immutable. On the contrary — as is seen in organic life at large — harmony would (it is contended) result from an ever-changing adjustment and readjustment of equilibrium between the multitudes of forces and influences, and this adjustment would be the easier to obtain as none of the forces would enjoy a special protection from the State.

If, it is contended, society were organised on these principles, man would not be limited in the free exercise of his powers in productive work by a capitalist monopoly, maintained by the State; nor would he be limited in the exercise of his will by a fear of punishment, or by obedience towards individuals or metaphysical entities, which both lead to depression of initiative and servility of mind. He would be guided in his actions by his own understanding, which necessarily would bear the impression of a free action and reaction between his own self and the ethical conceptions of his surroundings. Man would thus be enabled to obtain the full development of all his faculties, intellectual, artistic and moral, without being hampered by overwork for the monopolists, or by the servility and inertia of mind of the great number. He would thus be able to reach full *individualisation*, which is not possible either under the present system of *individualism*, or under any system of State Socialism in the so-called *Volksstaat* (Popular State).

The Anarchist writers consider, moreover, that their conception is not a Utopia, constructed on the a priori method, after a few desiderata have been taken as postulates. It is derived, they maintain, from an *analysis of tendencies* that are at work already, even though State Socialism may find a temporary favour with the reformers. The progress of modern technics, which wonderfully simplifies the production of all the necessaries of life; the growing spirit of independence, and the rapid spread of free initiative and free understanding in all branches of activity — including those which formerly were considered as the proper attribution of Church and State — are steadily reinforcing the no-government tendency.

As to their economical conceptions, the Anarchists, in common with all Socialists, of whom they constitute the left wing, maintain that the now prevailing system of private ownership in land, and our capitalist production for the sake of profits, represent a monopoly which runs against both the principles of justice and the dictates of utility. They are the main obstacle which prevents the successes of modern technics from being brought into the service of all, so as to produce general well-being. The Anarchists consider the wage system and capitalist production altogether as an obstacle to progress. But they point out also that the State was, and continues to be, the chief instrument for permitting the few to monopolise the land, and the capitalists to appropriate for themselves a quite disproportionate share of the yearly accumulated surplus of production. Consequently, while combatting the present monopolisation of land, and capitalism altogether, the Anarchists combat with the same energy the State, as the main support of that system. Not this or that special form, but the State altogether, whether it be a monarchy or even a republic governed by means of the referendum.

The State organisation, having always been, both in ancient and modern history (Macedonian empire, Roman empire, modern European states grown up on the ruins of the autonomous cities), the instrument for establishing monopolies in favour of the ruling minorities, cannot be made to work for the destruction of these monopolies. The Anarchists consider, therefore, that to hand over to the State all the main sources of economical life — the land, the mines, the railways, banking, insurance, and so on — as also the management of all the main branches of industry, in addition to all the functions already accumulated in its hands (education, State-supported religions, defence of the territory, &c), would mean to create a new instrument of tyranny. State capitalism would only increase the powers of bureaucracy and capitalism. True progress lies in the direction of decentralisation, both *territorial* and *functional*, in the development of the spirit of local and personal initiative, and of free federation from the simple to the compound, in lieu of the present hierarchy from the centre to the periphery.

In common with most Socialists, the Anarchists recognise that, like all evolution in nature, the slow evolution of society is followed from time to time by periods of accelerated evolution which are called revolutions; and they think that the era of revolutions is not yet closed. Periods of rapid changes will follow the periods of slow evolution, and these periods must be taken advantage of — not for increasing and widening the powers of the State, but for reducing them, through the organisation in every township or commune of the local groups of producers and consumers, as also the regional, and eventually the international, federations of these groups.

In virtue of the above principles the Anarchists refuse to be party to the present State organisation and to support it by infusing fresh blood into it. They do not seek to constitute, and invite the working men not to constitute, political parties in the parliaments. Accordingly, since the foundation of the International Working Men's Association in 1864-1866, they have endeavoured to promote their ideas directly amongst the labour organisations and to induce those unions to a direct struggle against capital, without placing their faith in parliamentary legislation.

The Historical Development of Anarchism
The conception of society just sketched, and the tendency which is its dynamic expression, have always existed in mankind, in opposition to the governing hierarchic conception and tendency — now the one and now the other taking the upper hand at different periods of history. To the former tendency we owe the evolution, by the masses themselves, of those institutions — the clan, the village community, the guild, the free medieval city — by means of which the masses resisted the encroachments of the conquerors and the power-seeking minorities. The same tendency asserted itself with great energy in the great religious movements of medieval times, especially in the early movements of the reform and its forerunners. At the same time it evidently found its expression in the writings of some thinkers, since the times of Lao-tse, although, owing to its non-scholastic and popular origin, it obviously found less sympathy among the scholars than the opposed tendency.

As has been pointed out by Prof. Adler in his *Geschichte des Sozialismus und Kommunismus*, Aristippus (b c. 430 BC), one of the founders of the Cyrenaic school, already taught that the wise must not give up their liberty to the State, and in reply to a question by Socrates he said that he did not desire to belong either to the governing or the governed class. Such an attitude, however, seems to have been dictated merely by an Epicurean attitude towards the life of the masses.

The best exponent of Anarchist philosophy in ancient Greece was Zeno (342-267 or 270 BC), from Crete, the founder of the Stoic philosophy, who distinctly opposed his conception of a free community without government to the State-Utopia of Plato. He repudiated the omnipotence of the State, its intervention and regimentation, and proclaimed the sovereignty of the moral law of the individual — remarking already that, while the necessary instinct of self-preservation leads man to egotism, nature has supplied a corrective to it by providing man with another instinct — that of sociability. When men are reasonable enough to follow their natural instincts, they will unite across the frontiers and constitute the Cosmos. They will have no need of law-courts or police, will have no temples and no public worship, and use no money — free gifts taking the place of the exchanges. Unfortunately, the writings of Zeno have not reached us and are only known through fragmentary quotations. However, the fact that his very wording is similar to the wording now in use, shows how deeply is laid the tendency of human nature of which he was the mouthpiece.

In medieval times we find the same views on the State expressed by the illustrious bishop of Alba, Marco Girolamo Vida, in his first dialogue *De dignitate reipublicae* (Ferd. Cavalli, in *Mem. dell' Istituto Veneto*, xiii; Dr E. Nys, *Researches in the History of Economics*). But it is especially in several early Christian movements, beginning with the ninth century in Armenia, and in the preachings of the early Hussites, particularly Chelčický, and the early Anabaptists, especially Johannes Denck (cf. Keller, *Ein Apostel der Wiedertäufer*), that one finds the same ideas forcibly expressed — special stress being laid of course on their moral aspects.

Rabelais and Fénelon, in their Utopias, have also expressed similar ideas, and they were also current in the eighteenth century amongst the French Encyclopaedists, as may be concluded from separate expressions occasionally met with in the writings of Rousseau, from Diderot's *Supplement* to the *Voyage* of Bougainville, and so on. However, in all probability such ideas could not be developed then, owing to the rigorous censorship of the Roman Catholic Church.

These ideas found their expression later during the great French Revolution. While the Jacobins did all in their power to centralise everything in the hands of the government, it appears now, from recently published documents, that the masses of the people, in their municipalities and 'sections', accomplished a considerable constructive work. They appropriated for themselves the election of the judges, the organisation of supplies and equipment for the army, as also for the large cities, work for the unemployed, the management of charities, and so on. They even tried to establish a direct correspondence between the 36,000 communes of France through the intermediary of a special board, outside the National Assembly (cf. Sigismund Lacroix, *Actes de la commune de Paris*).

It was Godwin, in his *Enquiry concerning Political Justice* (2 vols., 1793), who was the first to formulate the political and economical conceptions of Anarchism, even though he did not give that name to the ideas developed in his remarkable work. Laws, he wrote, are not a product of the wisdom of our ancestors: they are the product of their passions, their timidity, their jealousies and their ambition. The remedy they offer is worse than the evils they pretend to cure. If and only if all laws and courts were abolished, and the decisions in the arising contests were left to reasonable men chosen for that purpose, real justice would gradually be evolved. As to the State, Godwin frankly claimed its abolition. A society, he wrote, can perfectly well exist without any government: only the communities should be small and perfectly autonomous. Speaking of property, he stated that the rights of every one 'to every substance capable of contributing to the benefit of a human being' must be regulated by justice alone: the substance must go 'to him who most wants it'. His conclusion was Communism. Godwin, however, had not the courage to maintain his opinions. He entirely rewrote later on his chapter on property and mitigated his Communist views in the second edition of *Political Justice* (8vo, 1796).

Proudhon was the first to use, in 1840 (*Qu'est-ce que la propriété?* First Memoir), the name of Anarchy with application to the no-government state of society. The name of 'Anarchists' had been freely applied during the French Revolution by the Girondists to those revolutionaries who did not consider that the task of the Revolution was accomplished with the overthrow of Louis XVI, and insisted upon a series of economical measures being taken (the abolition of feudal rights without redemption, the return to the village communities of the communal lands enclosed since 1669, the limitation of landed property to 120 acres, progressive income-tax, the national organisation of exchanges on a just value basis, which already received a beginning of practical realisation, and so on).

Now Proudhon advocated a society without government, and

used the word Anarchy to describe it. Proudhon repudiated, as is known, all schemes of Communism, according to which mankind would be driven into communistic monasteries or barracks, as also all the schemes of State or State-aided Socialism which were advocated by Louis Blanc and the Collectivists. When he proclaimed in his first memoir on property that 'property is theft', he meant only property in its present, Roman-law, sense of 'right of use and abuse'; in property-rights, on the other hand, understood in the limited sense of *possession*, he saw the best protection against the encroachments of the State. At the same time he did not want violently to dispossess the present owners of land, dwelling-houses, mines, factories and so on. He preferred to attain the same end by rendering capital incapable of earning interest; and this he proposed to obtain by means of a national bank, based on the mutual confidence of all those who are engaged in production, who would agree to exchange among themselves their produces at cost-value, by means of labour cheques representing the hours of labour required to produce every given commodity. Under such a system, which Proudhon described as 'Mutuellisme', all the exchanges of services would be strictly equivalent. Besides, such a bank would be enabled to lend money without interest, levying only something like 1 per cent, or even less, for covering the cost of administration. Every one being thus enabled to borrow the money that would be required to buy a house, nobody would agree to pay any more a yearly rent for the use of it. A general 'social liquidation' would thus be rendered easy, without violent expropriation. The same applied to mines, railways, factories and so on.

In a society of this type the State would be useless. The chief relations between citizens would be based on free agreement and regulated by mere account-keeping. The contests might be settled by arbitration. A penetrating criticism of the State and all possible forms of government, and a deep insight into all economic problems, were well-known characteristics of Proudhon's work.

It is worth noticing that French mutualism had its precursor in England, in William Thompson, who began by mutualism before he became a Communist, and in his followers John Gray (*A Lecture on Human Happiness*, 1825; *The Social System*, 1831) and J. F. Bray (*Labour's Wrongs and Labour's Remedy*, 1839). It had also its precursor in America. Josiah Warren, who was born in 1798 (cf. W. Bailie, *Josiah Warren, the First American Anarchist*, Boston, 1900), and belonged to Owen's 'New Harmony', considered that the failure of this enterprise was chiefly due to the suppression of individuality and the lack of initiative and responsibility. These defects, he taught, were inherent to every scheme based upon authority and the community of goods. He advocated, therefore, complete individual liberty. In 1827 he opened in Cincinnati a little country store which was the first 'Equity Store', and which the people called 'Time Store', because it was based on labour being exchanged hour for hour in all sorts of produce. 'Cost — the limit of price', and consequently 'no interest', was the motto of his store, and later on of his 'Equity Village', near New York, which was still in existence in 1865. Mr Keith's 'House of Equity' at Boston, founded in 1855, is also worthy of notice.

While the economical, and especially the mutual-banking, ideas of Proudhon found supporters and even a practical application in the United States, his political conception of Anarchy found but little echo in France, where the Christian Socialism of Lamennais and the Fourierists, and the State Socialism of Louis Blanc and the followers of Saint-Simon, were dominating. These ideas found, however, some temporary support among the left-wing Hegelians in Germany, Moses Hess in 1843, and Karl Grün in 1845, who advocated Anarchism. Besides, the authoritarian Communism of Wilhelm Weitling having given origin to opposition amongst the Swiss working men, Wilhelm Marr gave expression to it in the 1840s.

On the other side, Individualist Anarchism found, also in Germany, its fullest expression in Max Stirner (Kaspar Schmidt), whose remarkable works (*Der Einzige und sein Eigenthum* and articles contributed to the *Rheinische Zeitung*) remained quite overlooked until they were brought into prominence by John Henry Mackay.

Prof. V. Basch, in a very able introduction to his interesting book, *L'Individualisme anarchiste: Max Stirner* (1904), has shown how the development of German philosophy from Kant to Hegel, and 'the absolute' of Schelling and the *Geist* of Hegel, necessarily provoked, when the anti-Hegelian revolt began, the preaching of the same 'absolute' in the camp of the rebels. This was done by Stirner, who advocated, not only a complete revolt against the State and against the servitude which authoritarian Communism would impose upon men, but also the full liberation of the individual from all social and moral bonds — the rehabilitation of the 'I', the supremacy of the individual, complete 'a-moralism', and the 'association of the egotists'. The final conclusion of that sort of Individualist Anarchism has been indicated by Prof. Basch. It maintains that the aim of all superior civilisation is, not to permit *all* members of the community to develop in a normal way, but to permit certain better-endowed individuals 'fully to develop', even at the cost of the happiness and the very existence of the mass of mankind. It is thus a return towards the most common individualism, advocated by all the would-be superior minorities, to which indeed man owes in his history precisely the State and the rest, which these individualists combat. Their individualism goes so far as to end in a negation of their own starting-point — to say nothing of the impossibility for the individual to attain a really full development in the conditions of oppression of the masses by the 'beautiful aristocracies'. His development would remain uni-lateral. This is why this direction of thought, notwithstanding its undoubtedly correct and useful advocacy of the full development of each individuality, finds a hearing only in limited artistic and literary circles.

Anarchism in the International Working Men's Association

A general depression in the propaganda of all factions of Socialism followed, as is known, after the defeat of the uprising of the Paris working men in June 1848 and the fall of the Republic. All the Socialist press was gagged during the reaction period, which lasted fully twenty years. Nevertheless, even Anarchist thought began to make some progress, namely in the writings of Bellegarrigue, Coeurderoy, and especially Joseph Déjacque (*Les Lazaréennes*, *L'Humanisphère*, an Anarchist-Communist Utopia, lately discovered and reprinted). The Socialist movement revived only after 1864, when some French working men, all 'mutualists', meeting in London during the Universal Exhibition with English followers of Robert Owen, founded the International Working Men's

Association. This association developed very rapidly and adopted a policy of direct economical struggle against capitalism, without interfering in the political parliamentary agitation, and this policy was followed until 1871. However, after the Franco-German War, when the International Association was prohibited in France after the uprising of the Commune, the German working men, who had received manhood suffrage for elections to the newly constituted imperial parliament, insisted upon modifying the tactics of the International, and began to build up a Social-Democratic political party. This soon led to a division in the Working Men's Association, and the Latin federations, Spanish, Italian, Belgian and Jurassic (France could not be represented), constituted among themselves a Federal union which broke entirely with the Marxist General Council of the International. Within these federations developed now what may be described as *modern Anarchism*. After the names of 'Federalists' and 'Anti-authoritarians' had been used for some time by these federations, the name of 'Anarchists', which their adversaries insisted upon applying to them, prevailed, and finally it was revindicated.

Bakunin soon became the leading spirit among these Latin federations for the development of the principles of Anarchism, which he did in a number of writings, pamphlets and letters. He demanded the complete abolition of the State, which — he wrote — is a product of religion, belongs to a lower state of civilisation, represents the negation of liberty, and spoils even that which it undertakes to do for the sake of general well-being. The State was an historically necessary evil, but its complete extinction will be, sooner or later, equally necessary. Repudiating all legislation, even when issuing from universal suffrage, Bakunin claimed for each nation, each region and each commune, full autonomy, so long as it is not a menace to its neighbours, and full independence for the individual, adding that one becomes really free only when, and in proportion as, all others are free. Free federations of the communes would constitute free nations.

As to his economical conceptions, Bakunin described himself, in common with his Federalist comrades of the International (César De Paepe, James Guillaume, Schwitzguébel), a 'Collectivist Anarchist' — not in the sense of Vidal and Pecqueur in the 1840s, or of their modern Social-Democratic followers, but to express a state of things in which all necessaries for production are owned in common by the Labour groups and the free communes, while the ways of retribution of labour, Communist or otherwise, would be settled by each group for itself. Social revolution, the near approach of which was foretold at that time by all Socialists, would be the means of bringing into life the new conditions.

The Jurassic, the Spanish, and the Italian federations and sections of the International Working Men's Association, as also the French, the German and the American Anarchist groups, were for the next years the chief centres of Anarchist thought and propaganda. They refrained from any participation in parliamentary politics, and always kept in close contact with the Labour organisations. However, in the second half of the 1880s and the early 1890s, when the influence of the Anarchists began to be felt in strikes, in the First of May demonstrations, where they promoted the idea of a general strike for an eight hours' day, and in the anti-militarist propaganda in the army, violent prosecutions were directed against them, especially in the Latin countries (including physical torture in the Barcelona Castle) and the United States (the execution of five Chicago Anarchists in 1887). Against these prosecutions the Anarchists retaliated by acts of violence which in their turn were followed by more executions from above, and new acts of revenge from below. This created in the general public the impression that violence is the substance of Anarchism, a view repudiated by its supporters, who hold that in reality violence is resorted to by all parties in proportion as their open action is obstructed by repression, and exceptional laws render them outlaws. (Cf. *Anarchism and Outrage*, by C. M. Wilson, and *Report of the Spanish Atrocities Committee*, in 'Freedom Pamphlets'; *A Concise History of the Great Trial of the Chicago Anarchists*, by Dyer Lum (New York, 1886); *The Chicago Martyrs: Speeches*, &c.)

Anarchism continued to develop, partly in the direction of Proudhonian 'Mutuellisme', but chiefly as Communist Anarchism, to which a third direction, Christian Anarchism, was added by Leo Tolstoy, and a fourth, which might be ascribed as literary Anarchism, began amongst some prominent modern writers.

The ideas of Proudhon, especially as regards mutual banking, corresponding with those of Josiah Warren, found a considerable following in the United States, creating quite a school, of which the main writers are Stephen Pearl Andrews, William Greene, Lysander Spooner (who began to write in 1850, and whose unfinished work, *Natural Law*, was full of promise), and several others, whose names will be found in Dr Nettlau's *Bibliographie de l'anarchie*.

A prominent position among the Individualist Anarchists in America has been occupied by Benjamin R. Tucker, whose journal *Liberty* was started in 1881 and whose conceptions are a combination of those of Proudhon with those of Herbert Spencer. Starting from the statement that Anarchists are egotists, strictly speaking, and that every group of individuals, be it a secret league of a few persons, or the Congress of the United States, has the right to oppress all mankind, provided it has the power to do so, that equal liberty for all and absolute equality ought to be the law, and 'mind every one your own business' is the unique moral law of Anarchism, Tucker goes on to prove that a general and thorough application of these principles would be beneficial and would offer no danger, because the powers of every individual would be limited by the exercise of the equal rights of all others. He further indicated (following H. Spencer) the difference which exists between the encroachment on somebody's rights and resistance to such encroachment; between domination and defence: the former being equally condemnable, whether it be encroachment of a criminal upon an individual, or the encroachment of one upon all others, or of all others upon one; while resistance to encroachment is defensible and necessary. For their self-defence, both the citizen and the group have the right to any violence, including capital punishment. Violence is also justified for enforcing the duty of keeping an agreement. Tucker thus follows Spencer, and, like him, opens (in the present writer's opinion) the way for reconstituting under the heading of 'defence' all the functions of the State. His criticism of the present State is very searching, and his defence of the rights of the individual very powerful. As regards his economical views B. R. Tucker follows Proudhon.

The Individualist Anarchism of the American Proudhonians finds, however, but little sympathy amongst the working masses.

Those who profess it — they are chiefly 'intellectuals' — soon realise that the *individualisation* they so highly praise is not attainable by individual efforts, and either abandon the ranks of the Anarchists, and are driven into the Liberal individualism of the classical economists, or they retire into a sort of Epicurean a-moralism, or super-man theory, similar to that of Stirner and Nietzsche. The great bulk of the Anarchist working men prefer the Anarchist-Communist ideas which have gradually evolved out of the Anarchist Collectivism of the International Working Men's Association. To this direction belong — to name only the better-known exponents of Anarchism — Eliśee Reclus, Jean Grave, Sébastien Faure, Emile Pouget in France; Errico Malatesta and Covelli in Italy; R. Mella, A. Lorenzo, and the mostly unknown authors of many excellent manifestos in Spain; John Most amongst the Germans; Spies, Parsons and their followers in the United States, and so on; while Domela Nieuwenhuis occupies an intermediate position in Holland. The chief Anarchist papers which have been published since 1880 also belong to that direction; while a number of Anarchists of this direction have joined the so-called Syndicalist movement — the French name for the non-political Labour movement, devoted to direct struggle with capitalism, which has lately become so prominent in Europe.

As one of the Anarchist-Communist direction, the present writer for many years endeavoured to develop the following ideas: to show the intimate, logical connection which exists between the modern philosophy of natural sciences and Anarchism; to put Anarchism on a scientific basis by the study of the tendencies that are apparent now in society and may indicate its further evolution; and to work out the basis of Anarchist ethics. As regards the substance of Anarchism itself, it was Kropotkin's aim to prove that Communism — at least partial — has more chances of being established than Collectivism, especially in communes taking the lead, and that Free, or Anarchist, Communism is the only form of Communism that has any chance of being accepted in civilised societies; Communism and Anarchy are therefore two terms of evolution which complete each other, the one rendering the other possible and acceptable. He has tried, moreover, to indicate how, during a revolutionary period, a large city — if its inhabitants have accepted the idea — could organise itself on the lines of Free Communism; the city guaranteeing to every inhabitant dwelling, food and clothing to an extent corresponding to the comfort now available to the middle classes only, in exchange for a half-day's, or a five-hours' work; and how all those things which would be considered as luxuries might be obtained by every one if he joins for the other half of the day all sorts of free associations pursuing all possible aims — educational, literary, scientific, artistic, sports and so on. In order to prove the first of these assertions he has analysed the possibilities of agriculture and industrial work, both being combined with brain work. And in order to elucidate the main factors of human evolution, he has analysed the part played in history by the popular constructive agencies of mutual aid and the historical role of the State.

Without naming himself an Anarchist, Leo Tolstoy, like his predecessors in the popular religious movements of the fifteenth and sixteenth centuries, Chelčický, Denck, and many others, took the Anarchist position as regards the State and property rights, deducing his conclusions from the general spirit of the teachings of the Christ and from the necessary dictates of reason. With all the might of his talent he made (especially in *The Kingdom of God is Within You*) a powerful criticism of the Church, the State and law altogether, and especially of the present property laws. He describes the State as the domination of the wicked ones, supported by brutal force. Robbers, he says, are far less dangerous than a well-organised government. He makes a searching criticism of the prejudices which are current now concerning the benefits conferred upon men by the Church, the State and the existing distribution of property, and from the teachings of the Christ he deduces the rule of non-resistance and the absolute condemnation of all wars. His religious arguments are, however, so well combined with arguments borrowed from a dispassionate observation of the present evils, that the Anarchist portions of his works appeal to the religious and the non-religious reader alike.

It would be impossible to represent here, in a short sketch, the penetration, on the one hand, of Anarchist ideas into modern literature, and the influence, on the other hand, which the libertarian ideas of the best contemporary writers have exercised upon the development of Anarchism. One ought to consult the ten big volumes of the *Supplément littéraire* to the paper *La Révolte* and later the *Temps Nouveaux*, which contain reproductions from the works of hundreds of modern authors expressing Anarchist ideas, in order to realise how closely Anarchism is connected with all the intellectual movement of our own times. J. S. Mill's *On Liberty*, Spencer's *The Man versus the State*, Guyau's *Morality without Obligation or Sanction*, and Fouillée's *La morale, l'art et la réligion*, the works of Multatuli (E. Douwes Dekker), Richard Wagner's *Art and Revolution*, the works of Nietzsche, Emerson, W. Lloyd Garrison, Thoreau, Alexander Herzen, Edward Carpenter and so on; and in the domain of fiction, the dramas of Ibsen, the poetry of Walt Whitman, Tolstoy's *War and Peace*, Zola's *Paris* and *Le Travail*, the latest works of Merezhkovsky, and an infinity of works of less-known authors — are full of ideas which show how closely Anarchism is interwoven with the work that is going on in modern thought in the same direction of enfranchisement of man from the bonds of the State as well as from those of capitalism.

Bibliography

Anarchism, which was written in 1905, first appeared in 1910 in the first volume of the eleventh edition of the *Encyclopaedia Britannica* (which was edited by Hugh Chisholm and published by the Cambridge University Press in 1910-1911), signed 'P.A.K.'. It replaced a short article in the tenth edition of 1902 by Henry Demarest Lloyd, the American progressive journalist who had campaigned for the Haymarket Martyrs in 1887 (and who died in 1903).

Kropotkin's article continued to appear for half a century in successive editions and impressions of the *Encyclopaedia Britannica* (published in the United States), with various deletions, alterations and additions. In the fourteenth edition of 1929, it was supplemented with a postscript by Harold J. Laski, the Anglo-American politician and political scientist who was a leading member of the British Labour Party but sympathetic to anarchism. This remained unaltered until the impression of 1957, when it was replaced with a new postscript by Kazimierz Smogorzewski, an Anglo-Polish journalist.

In the impression of 1960, Kropotkin's article and Smogorzewski's postscript were replaced with a new and up-to-date but derivative and shorter article by Karl Wolfgang Deutsch, an American academic. In the fifteenth edition (the so-called *New Encyclopaedia Britannica*, which was an entirely fresh version edited by Warren E. Preece and published in Chicago in 1974), there was at last a completely new full-length article by George Woodcock, the Anglo-Canadian critic and biographer who had been a leading member of the British anarchist movement and was the author of the best-known book on the subject, *Anarchism* (1962, 1963, 1974, 1986).

Kropotkin's article has frequently been reprinted or translated as a separate pamphlet or included in collections of his writings or anthologies of anarchist writings, but these editions have invariably reproduced the old errors and have frequently introduced new ones. The present edition follows the original version of 1910, with the omission of a long editorial footnote listing various assassinations attributed to anarchists and of a long bibliography of publications about anarchism, and with the minimum of alterations to correct the factual errors (especially in the names of individuals and the titles of publications) and to regularise spelling, capitalisation and punctuation.

2
ANARCHIST COMMUNISM:
Its Basis and Principles

I

ANARCHY, the No-Government system of Socialism, has a double origin. It is an outgrowth of the two great movements of thought in the economical and the political fields which characterise our century, and especially its second part. In common with all Socialists, the Anarchists hold that the private ownership of land, capital, and machinery has had its time; that it is condemned to disappear; and that all requisites for production must, and will, become the common property of society, and be managed in common by the producers of wealth. And, in common with the most advanced representatives of political Radicalism, they maintain that the ideal of the political organisation of society is a condition of things where the functions of government are reduced to a minimum, and the individual recovers his full liberty of initiative and action for satisfying, by means of free groups and federations — freely constituted — all the infinitely varied needs of the human being. As regards Socialism, most of the Anarchists arrive at its ultimate conclusion, that is, at a complete negation of the wage system and at Communism. And with reference to political organisation, by giving a further development to the above-mentioned part of the Radical programme, they arrive at the conclusion that the ultimate aim of society is the reduction of the functions of government to nil — that is, to a society without government, to An-archy. The Anarchists maintain, moreover, that such being the ideal of social and political organisation, they must not remit it to future centuries, but that only those changes in our social organisation which are in accordance with the above double ideal, and constitute an approach to it, will have a chance of life and be beneficial for the commonwealth.

As to the method followed by the Anarchist thinker, it entirely differs from that followed by the Utopists. The Anarchist thinker does not resort to metaphysical conceptions (like 'natural rights', the 'duties of the State' and so on) to establish what are, in his opinion, the best conditions for realising the greatest happiness of humanity. He follows, on the contrary, the course traced by the modern philosophy of evolution — without entering, however, the slippery route of mere analogies so often resorted to by Herbert Spencer. He studies human society as it is now and was in the past; and, without either endowing men altogether, or separate individuals, with superior qualities which they do not possess, he merely considers society as an aggregation of organisms trying to find out the best ways of combining the wants of the individual with those of cooperation for the welfare of the species. He studies society and tries to discover its *tendencies*, past and present, its growing needs, intellectual and economical, and in his ideal he merely points out in which direction evolution goes. He distinguishes between the real wants and tendencies of human aggregations and the accidents (want of knowledge, migrations, wars, conquests) which have prevented these tendencies from being satisfied, or temporarily paralysed them. And he concludes that the two most prominent, although often unconscious, tendencies throughout our history have been: a tendency towards integrating labour for the production of all riches in common, so as finally to render it impossible to discriminate the part of the common production due to the separate individual; and a tendency towards the fullest freedom of the individual in the prosecution of all aims, beneficial both for himself and for society at large. The ideal of the Anarchist is thus a mere summing-up of what he considers to be the next phase of evolution. It is no longer a matter of faith; it is a matter for scientific discussion.

In fact, one of the leading features of our century is the growth of Socialism and the rapid spreading of Socialist views among the working classes. How could it be otherwise? We have witnessed during the last seventy years an unparalleled sudden increase of our powers of production, resulting in an accumulation of wealth which has outstripped the most sanguine expectations. But, owing to our wage system, this increase of wealth — due to the combined efforts of men of science, of managers, and workmen as well — has resulted only in an unprevented accumulation of wealth in the hands of the owners of capital; while an increase of misery for great numbers, and an insecurity of life for all, have been the lot of the workmen. The unskilled labourers, in continuous search for labour, are falling into an unheard-of destitution; and even the best-paid artisans and skilled workmen, who undoubtedly are living now a more comfortable life than before, labour under the permanent menace of being thrown, in their turn, into the same conditions as the unskilled paupers, in consequence of some of the continuous and unavoidable fluctuations of industry and caprices of capital. The chasm between the modern millionaire who squanders the produce of human labour in a gorgeous and vain luxury, and the pauper reduced to a miserable and insecure existence, is thus growing wider and wider, so as to break the very unity of society — the harmony of its life — and to endanger the progress of its further development. At the same time, working men are less and less inclined patiently to endure this division of society into two classes, as they themselves become more and more conscious of the wealth-producing power of modern industry, of the part played by labour in the production of wealth, and of their own capacities of organisation. In proportion as all classes of the community take a more lively part in public affairs, and knowledge spreads among the masses, their longing for equality becomes stronger, and their demands for social reorganisation become louder and louder: they can be ignored no more. The worker claims his share in the riches he produces; he claims his share in the management of production; and he claims not only some additional well-being, but also his full rights in the higher enjoyments of science and art. These claims, which formerly were uttered only by the social reformer, begin now to be made by a daily growing minority of those who work in the factory or till the acre; and they so conform to our feelings of justice, that they find support in a daily growing minority amidst the privileged classes themselves. Socalism becomes thus *the* idea of the nineteenth century; and neither coercion nor pseudo-reforms can stop its further growth.

Much hope of improvement was placed, of course, in the extension of political rights to the working classes. But these concessions, unsupported as they were by corresponding changes in economical relations, proved delusory. They did not materially improve the conditions of the great bulk of the workmen. Therefore, the watchword of Socialism is: 'Economical freedom, as the only secure basis for political freedom.' And as long as the present wage system, with all its bad consequences, remains unaltered, the Socialist watchword will continue to inspire the workmen. Socialism will continue to grow until it has realised its programme.

Side by side with this great movement of thought in economical matters, a like movement has been going on with regard to political rights, political organisation, and the functions of government. Government has been submitted to the same criticism as Capital. While most of the Radicals saw in universal suffrage and republican institutions the last word of political wisdom, a further step was made by the few. The very functions of government and the State, as also their relations to the individual, were submitted to a sharper and deeper criticism. Representative government having been tried by experiment on a wide field, its defects became more and more prominent. It became obvious that these defects are not merely accidental, but inherent in the system itself. Parliament and its executive proved to be unable to attend to all the numberless affairs of the community and to conciliate the varied and often opposite interests of the separate parts of a State. Election proved unable to find out the men who might represent a nation, and manage, otherwise than in a party spirit, the affairs they are compelled to legislate upon. These defects became so striking that the very principles of the representative system were criticised and their justness doubted. Again, the dangers of a centralised government became still more conspicuous when the Socialists came to the front and asked for a further increase of the powers of government by entrusting it with the management of the immense field covered now by the economical relations between individuals. The question was asked, whether a government, entrusted with the management of industry and trade, would not become a permanent danger for liberty and peace, and whether it even would be able to be a good manager.

The Socialists of the earlier part of this century did not fully realise the immense difficulties of the problem. Convinced as they were of the necessity of economical reforms, most of them took no notice of the need of freedom for the individual; and we have had social reformers ready to submit society to any kind of theocracy, dictatorship, or even Caesarism, in order to obtain reforms in a Socialist sense. Therefore we have seen, in this country and also on the Continent, the division of men of advanced opinions into political Radicals and Socialists — the former looking with distrust on the latter, as they saw in them a danger for the political liberties which have been won by the civilised nations after a long series of struggles. And even now, when the Socialists all over Europe are becoming political parties, and profess the democratic faith, there remains among most impartial men a well-founded fear of the *Volksstaat* or 'Popular State' being as great a danger for liberty as any form of autocracy, if its government be entrusted with the management of all the social organisation, including the production and distribution of wealth.

The evolution of the last forty years has prepared, however, the way for showing the necessity and possibility of a higher form of social organisation which may guarantee economical freedom without reducing the individual to the role of a slave to the State. The origins of government have been carefully studied, and all metaphysical conceptions as to its divine or 'social contract' derivation having been laid aside, it appears that it is among us of a relatively modern origin, and that its powers have grown precisely in proportion as the division of society into the privileged and unprivileged classes was growing in the course of ages. Representative government has also been reduced to its real value — that of an instrument which has rendered services in the struggle against autocracy, but not an ideal of free political organisation. As to the system of philosophy which saw in the State (the *Kulturstaat*) a leader of progress, it was more and more shaken as it became evident that progress is the more effective when it is not checked by State interference. It has thus become obvious that a further advance in social life does not lie in the direction of a further concentration of power and regulative functions in the hands of a governing body, but in the direction of decentralisation, both territorial and functional — in a subdivision of public functions with respect both to their sphere of action and to the character of the functions; it is in the abandonment to the initiative of freely constituted groups of all those functions which are now considered as the functions of government.

This current of thought has found its expression not merely in literature, but also, to a limited extent, in life. The uprise of the Paris Commune, followed by that of the Commune of Cartagena — a movement of which the historical bearing seems to have been quite overlooked in this country — opened a new page of history. If we analyse not only this movement in itself, but also the impression it left in the minds and the tendencies manifested during the communal revolution, we must recognise in it an indication showing that, in the future, human agglomerations which are more advanced in their social development will try to start an independent life; and that they will endeavour to convert the more backward parts of a nation by example, instead of imposing their opinions by law and force, or submitting themselves to the majority-rule, which always is a mediocrity-rule. At the same time the failure of representative government within the Commune itself proved that self-government and self-administration must be carried further than in a merely territorial sense; to be effective they must also be carried into the various functions of life within the free community; a merely territorial limitation of the sphere of action of government will not do — representative government being as deficient in a city as it is in a nation. Life gave thus a further point in favour of the no-government theory, and a new impulse to anarchist thought.

Anarchists recognise the justice of both the just-mentioned tendencies towards economical and political freedom, and see in them two different manifestations of the very same need of equality which constitutes the very essence of all struggles mentioned by history. Therefore, in common with all Socialists, the Anarchist says to the political reformer: 'No substantial reform in the sense of political equality, and no limitation of the powers of government, can be made as long as society is divided into two hostile camps, and the labourer remains, economically speaking, a serf to his employer.' But to the Popular State Socialist we say also: 'You cannot modify the existing conditions of property without deeply modifying at the same time the political organisation. You must limit the powers of government and renounce Parliamentary rule. To each new economical phase of life corresponds a new political phase. Absolute monarchy — that is, Court-rule — corresponded to the system of serfdom. Representative government corresponds to Capital-rule. Both, however, are class-rule. But in a society where the distinction between capitalist and labourer has disappeared, there is no need of such a government; it would be an anachronism, a nuisance. Free workers would require a free organisation, and this cannot have another basis than free agreement and free cooperation, without sacrificing the autonomy of the individual to the all-pervading interference of the State. The no-capitalist system implies the no-government system.'

Meaning thus the emancipation of man from the oppressive powers of capitalist and government as well, the system of Anarchy becomes a synthesis of the two powerful currents of thought which characterise our century.

In arriving at these conclusions Anarchy proves to be in accordance with the conclusions arrived at by the philosophy of evolution. By bringing to light the plasticity of organisation, the philosophy of evolution has shown the admirable adaptivity of organisms to their conditions of life, and the ensuing development of such faculties as render more complete both the adaptations of the aggregates to their surroundings and those of each of the constituent parts of the aggregate to the needs of free cooperation. It has familiarised us with the circumstance that throughout organic nature the capacities for life in common grow in proportion as the integration of organisms into compound aggregates becomes more and more complete; and it has enforced thus the opinion already expressed by social moralists as to the perfectibility of human nature. It has shown us that, in the long run of the struggle for existence, 'the fittest' will prove to be those who combine intellectual knowledge with the knowledge necessary for the production of wealth, and not those who are now the richest because they, or their ancestors, have been momentarily the strongest. By showing that the 'struggle for existence' must be conceived, not merely in its restricted sense of a struggle between individuals for the means of subsistence, but in its wider sense of adaptation of all individuals of the species to the best conditions for the survival of the species, as well as for the greatest possible sum of life and happiness for each and all, it has permitted us to deduce the laws of moral science from the social needs and habits of mankind. It has shown us the infinitesimal part played by positive law in moral evolution, and the immense part played by the natural growth of altruistic feelings, which develop as soon as the conditions of life favour their growth. It has thus enforced the opinion of social reformers as to the necessity of modifying the conditions of life for improving man, instead of trying to improve human nature by moral teachings while life works in an opposite direction. Finally, by studying human society from the biological point of view, it has come to the conclusions arrived at by Anarchists from the study of history and present tendencies, as to further progress being in the line of socialisation of wealth and integrated labour, combined with the fullest possible freedom of the individual.

It is not a mere coincidence that Herbert Spencer, whom we may consider as a pretty fair expounder of the philosophy of evolution, has been brought to conclude, with regard to political organisation, that 'that form of society towards which we are progressing' is 'one in which *government* will be reduced to the smallest amount possible, and *freedom* increased to the greatest amount possible.'[1] When he opposes in these words the conclusions of his synthetic

---

1 *Essays*, Vol III. I am fully aware that in the very same *Essays*, a few pages further, Herbert Spencer destroys the force of the foregoing statement by the following words: 'Not only do I contend', he says, 'that the restraining power of the State over individuals and bodies, or classes of individuals, is requisite, but I have contended that it should be exercised much more effectually and carried much farther than at present' (p.145). And although he tries to establish a distinction between the (desirable) negatively regulative and the (undesirable) positively regulative functions of government, we know that no such distinction can be established in political life, and that the former necessarily lead to, and even imply, the latter. But we must distinguish between the system of philosophy and its interpreter. All we can say is that Herbert Spencer does not endorse all the conclusions which ought to be drawn from his system of philosophy.

philosophy to those of Auguste Comte, he arrives at very nearly the same conclusion as Proudhon[2] and Bakunin[3]. More than that, the very methods of argumentation and the illustrations resorted to by Herbert Spencer (daily supply of food, post-office, and so on) are the same which we find in the writings of the Anarchists. The channels of thought were the same, although both were unaware of each other's endeavours.

Again, when Mr Spencer so powerfully, and even not without a touch of passion, argues (in his Appendix to the third edition of the *Data of Ethics*) that human societies are marching towards a state when a further identification of altruism with egoism will be made 'in the sense that personal gratification will come from the gratification of others'; when he says that 'we are shown, undeniably, that it is a perfectly possible thing for organisms to become so adjusted to the requirements of their lives, that energy expended for the general welfare may not only be adequate to check energy expended for the individual welfare, but may come to subordinate it so far as to leave individual welfare no greater part than is necessary for maintenance of individual life' — provided the conditions for such relations between the individual and the community be maintained[4] — he derives from the study of nature the very same conclusions as the forerunners of Anarchy, Fourier and Robert Owen, derived from a study of human character.

When we see further Mr Bain so forcibly elaborating the theory of moral habits, and the French philosopher, M Guyau, unveiling in a most remarkable work the basis of *Morality without Obligation or Sanction*; when J. S. Mill so sharply criticises representative government and discusses the problem of liberty, although failing to establish its necessary conditions; when modern biology brings us to understand the importance of free cooperation and mutual aid in the animal world; when Lewis Morgan (in *Ancient Society*) shows

---

2 *Idée générale sur la Révolution au XIXe siècle*; and *Confessions d'un révolutionnaire*.

3 *Lettres à un Français sur la crise actuelle*; *L'Empire knouto-germanique*; *The State Idea and Anarchy* (Russian).

4 Pages 300 to 302. In fact, the whole of this chapter, which did not appear in the first two editions, ought to be quoted.

us the parasitical development of State and property amidst the free institutions of our earliest ancestors, and modern history follows the same lines of argumentation — when, in short, every year, by bringing some new arguments to the philosophy of evolution, adds at the same time some new arguments to the philosophy of Anarchy — we must recognise that this last, although differing as to its starting-point, follows the same sound methods of scientific investigation. Our confidence in its conclusions is still more increased. The difference between Anarchists and the just-named philosophers may be immense as to the presumed speed of evolution, and as to the line of conduct which one ought to assume as soon as he has had an insight into the aims towards which society is marching. No attempt, however, has been made scientifically to determine the ratio of evolution, nor has the chief element of the problem (the state of mind of the masses) ever been taken into account by the evolutionist philosophers. As to bringing one's action into accordance with his philosophical conceptions, we know that, unhappily, intellect and will are too often separated by a chasm not to be filled by mere philosophical speculations, however deep and elaborate.

There is, however, between the just-named philosophers and the Anarchists a wide difference on one point of primordial importance. This difference is the stranger as it arises on a point which might be discussed figures in hand, and which constitutes the very basis of all further deductions, as it belongs to what biological sociology would describe as the physiology of nutrition.

There is, in fact, a widely spread fallacy, maintained by Mr Spencer and many others, as to the causes of the misery which we see round about us. It was affirmed forty years ago, and it is affirmed now by Mr Spencer and his followers, that misery in civilised society is due to our insufficient production, or rather to the circumstance that 'population presses upon the means of subsistence'. It would be of no use to inquire into the origin of such a misrepresentation of facts, which might be easily verified. It may have its origin in inherited misconceptions which have nothing to do with the philosophy of evolution. But to be maintained and advocated by philosophers, there must be, in the conceptions of these philosophers, some confusion as to the different aspects of the struggle for existence. Sufficient importance is not given to the difference between the struggle which goes on among organisms which do *not* cooperate for providing the means of subsistence, and those which *do* so. In this last case again there must be some confusion between those aggregates whose members find their means of subsistence in the ready-made produce of the vegetable and animal kingdom, and those whose members artificially grow their means of subsistence and are enabled to increase (to a yet unknown amount) the productivity of each spot of the surface of the globe. Hunters who hunt, each of them for his own sake, and hunters who unite into societies for hunting, stand quite differently with regard to the means of subsistence as they are in nature, and to civilised men who grow their food and produce by machinery all requisites for a comfortable life. In this last case — the stock of potential energy in nature being little short of infinite in comparison with the present population of the globe — the means of availing ourselves of the stock of energy are increased and perfected precisely in proportion to the density of population and to the previously accumulated stock of technical knowledge; so that for human beings who are in possession of scientific knowledge, and cooperate for the artificial production of the means of subsistence and comfort, the law is quite the reverse of that of Malthus. The accumulation of means of subsistence and comfort is going on at a much speedier rate than the increase of population. The only conclusion which we can deduce from the laws of evolution and of multiplication of effects is that the available amount of means of subsistence increases at a rate which increases itself in proportion as population becomes denser — unless it be artificially (and temporarily) checked by some defects of social organisation. As to our *powers* of production (our potential production), they increase at a still speedier rate in proportion as scientific knowledge grows, the means for spreading it are rendered easier, and inventive genius is stimulated by all previous inventions.

If the fallacy as to the pressure of population on the means of subsistence could be maintained a hundred years ago, it can be maintained no more, since we have witnessed the effects of science on industry, and the enormous increase of our productive powers during the last hundred years. We know, in fact, that while the growth of population in England has been from 16½ millions in 1844 to 26¾ millions in 1883, showing thus an increase of 62 per cent, the growth of national wealth (as testified by Schedule A of the Income Tax Act) has increased twice as fast; it has grown from 221 to 507½ millions — that is, by 130 per cent. And we know that the same increase of wealth has taken place in France, where population remains almost stationary, and that it has gone on at a still speedier rate in the United States, where population is increasing every year by immigration.

But the figures just mentioned, while showing the real increase of production, give only a faint idea of what our production might be under a more reasonable economical organisation. We know well that the owners of capital, while trying to produce more wares with fewer 'hands', are continually endeavouring at the same time to limit the production, in order to sell at higher prices. When the profits of a concern are going down, the owner of the capital limits the production, or totally suspends it, and prefers to engage his capital in foreign loans or shares in Patagonian gold-mines. Just now there are plenty of pitmen in England who ask for nothing better than to be permitted to extract coal and supply with cheap fuel the households where children are shivering before empty chimneys. There are thousands of weavers who ask for nothing better than to weave stuffs in order to replace the ragged dress of the poor with decent clothing. And so in all branches of industry. How can we talk about a want of means of subsistence when thousands of factories lie idle in Great Britain alone; and when there are, just now, thousands and thousands of unemployed in London alone; thousands of men who would consider themselves happy if they were permitted to transform (under the guidance of experienced agriculturists) the clay of Middlesex into a rich soil, and to cover with cornfields and orchards the acres of meadow-land which now yields only a few pounds' worth of hay? But they are prevented from doing so by the owners of the land, of the weaving factory, and of the coal-mine, because capital finds it more advantageous to supply the Khedive with harems and the Russian Government with 'strategic railways' and Krupp guns. Of course the maintenance of harems *pays*: it gives 10 or 15 per cent on the capital, while the extraction of coal does not pay — that is, it brings 3 or 5 per cent — and that is a sufficient reason for limiting the production and permitting would-be economists to indulge in reproaches to the working classes as to their too rapid multiplication!

Here we have instances of a direct and conscious limitation of production, due to the circumstance that the requisites for production belong to the few, and that these few have the right of disposing of them at their will, without caring about the interests of the community. But there is also the indirect and unconscious limitation of production — that which results from squandering the produce of human labour in luxury, instead of applying it to a further increase of production.

This last cannot even be estimated in figures, but a walk through the rich shops of any city and a glance at the manner in which money is squandered now, can give an approximate idea of this indirect limitation. When a rich man spends a thousand pounds for his stables, he squanders five to six thousand days of human labour, which might be used, under a better social organisation, for supplying with comfortable homes those who are compelled to live now in dens. And when a lady spends a hundred pounds for her dress, we cannot but say that she squanders, at least, two years of human labour, which, again under a better organisation, might have supplied a hundred women with decent dresses, and much more if applied to a further improvement of the instruments of production. Preachers thunder against luxury, because it is shameful to squander money for feeding and sheltering hounds and horses, when thousands live in the East End on sixpence a day, and other thousands have not even their miserable sixpence every day. But the economist sees more than that in our modern luxury: when millions of days of labour are spent every year for the satisfaction of the stupid vanity of the rich, he says that so many millions of workers have been diverted from the manufacture of those useful instruments which would permit us to decuple and centuple our present production of means of subsistence and of requisites for comfort.

In short, if we take into account both the real and the potential increase of our wealth, and consider both the direct and indirect limitation of production, which are unavoidable under our present economical system, we must recognise that the supposed 'pressure of population on the means of subsistence' is a mere fallacy, repeated, like many other fallacies, without even taking the trouble of submitting it to a moment's criticism. The causes of the present social disease must be sought elsewhere.

Let us take a civilised country. The forests have been cleared, the swamps drained. Thousands of roads and railways intersect it in all directions; the rivers have been rendered navigable, and the seaports are of easy access. Canals connect the seas. The rocks have been pierced by deep shafts; thousands of manufactures cover the land. Science has taught man how to use the energy of nature for the satisfaction of his needs. Cities have slowly grown in the course of ages, and treasures of science and art are accumulated in these centres of civilisation. But — who has made all these marvels?

The combined efforts of scores of generations have contributed towards the achievement of these results. The forests have been cleared centuries ago; millions of men have spent years and years of labour in draining the swamps, in tracing the roads, in building the railways. Other millions have built the cities and created the civilisation we boast of. Thousands of inventors, mostly unknown, mostly dying in poverty and neglect, have elaborated the machinery in which man admires his genius. Thousands of writers, philosophers and men of science, supported by many thousands of compositors, printers, and other labourers whose name is legion, have contributed to elaborating and spreading knowledge, to dissipating errors, to creating the atmosphere of scientific thought, without which the marvels of our century never would have been brought to life. The genius of a Mayer and a Grove, the patient work of a Joule, surely have done more to give a new start to modern industry than all the capitalists of the world; but these men of genius themselves are, in their turn, the children of industry: thousands of engines had to transform heat into mechanical force, and mechanical force into sound, light, and electricity — and they had to do so for years, every day, under the eyes of humanity — before some of our contemporaries proclaimed the mechanical origin of heat and the correlation of physical forces, and before we ourselves became prepared to listen to them and understand their teachings. Who knows for how many decades we should continue to be ignorant of this theory which now revolutionises industry, were it not for the inventive powers and skill of those unknown workers who have improved the steam-engine, who have brought all its parts to perfection, so as to make steam more manageable than a horse, and to render the use of the engine nearly universal? But the same is true with regard to each smallest part of our machinery. In each machine, however simple, we may read a whole history — a long history of sleepless nights, of delusions and joys, of partial inventions and partial improvements which have brought it to its present state. Nay, nearly every new machine is a synthesis, a result of thousands of partial inventions made, not only in one special department of machinery, but in all departments of the wide field of mechanics.

Our cities, connected by roads and brought into easy communication with all peopled parts of the globe, are the growth of centuries; and each house in these cities, each factory, each shop, derives its value, its very *raison d'être*, from the fact that it is situated on a spot of the globe where thousands or millions have gathered together. Every smallest part of the immense whole which we call the wealth of civilised nations derives its value precisely from being a part of this whole. What would be the value of an immense London shop or warehouse were it not situated precisely in London, which has become the gathering spot for five millions of human beings? And what the value of our coal-pits, our manufactures, our shipbuilding yards, were it not for the immense traffic which goes on across the seas, for the railways which transport mountains of merchandise, for the cities which number their inhabitants by millions? Who is, then, the individual who has the right to step forward and, laying his hand on the smallest part of this immense whole, to say, '*I* have produced this; it belongs to *me*'? And how can we discriminate, in this immense interwoven whole, the part which the isolated individual may appropriate to himself with the slightest approach to justice? Houses and streets, canals and railways, machines and works of art, all these have been created by the combined efforts of generations past and present, of men living on these islands and men living thousands of miles away.

But it has happened in the long run of ages that everything which permits men further to increase their production, or even to continue it, has been appropriated by the few. The land, which derives its value precisely from its being necessary for an ever-increasing population, belongs to the few, who may prevent the community from cultivating it. The coal-pits, which represent the labour of generations, and which also derive their value from the wants of the manufactures and railroads, from the immense trade carried on and the density of population (what is the value of coal-layers in Transbaikalia?), belong again to the few, who have even the right of stopping the extraction of coal if they choose to give another use to their capital. The lace-weaving machine, which represents, in its present state of perfection, the work of three generations of Lancashire weavers, belongs again to the few; and if the grandsons of the very same weaver who invented the first lace-weaving machine claim their right to bring one of these machines into motion, they will be told, 'Hands off! this machine does not belong to you!' The railroads, which mostly would be useless heaps of iron if Great Britain had not its present dense population, its industry, trade, and traffic, belong again to the few — to a few shareholders, who may not even know where the railway is situated which brings them a yearly income larger than that of a medieval king; and if the children of those people who died by thousands in digging the tunnels should gather and go — a ragged and starving crowd — to ask bread or work from the shareholders, they would be met with bayonets and bullets.

Who is the sophist who will dare to say that such an organisation is just? But what is unjust cannot be beneficial to mankind; and *it is not.* In consequence of this monstrous organisation, the son of a workman, when he is able to work, finds no acre to till, no machine to set in motion, unless he agrees to sell his labour for a sum inferior to its real value. His father and grandfather have contributed to drain the field, or erect the factory, to the full extent of their capacities — and nobody can do more than that — but he comes into the world more destitute than a savage. If he resorts to agriculture, he will be permitted to cultivate a plot of land, but on the condition that he gives up one quarter of his crop to the landlord. If he resorts to industry, he will be permitted to work, but on the condition that out of the thirty shillings he has produced, ten shillings or more will be pocketed by the owner of the machine. We cry out against the feudal barons who did not permit anyone to settle on the land otherwise than on payment of one quarter of the crops to the lord of the manor; but we continue to do as they did — we extend their system. The forms have changed, but the essence has remained the same. And the workman is compelled to accept the feudal conditions which we call 'free contract', because nowhere will he find better conditions. Everything has been appropriated by somebody; he *must* accept the bargain, or starve.

Owing to this circumstance our production takes a wrong turn. It takes no care of the needs of the community; its only aim is to increase the profits of the capitalist. Therefore — the continuous fluctuations of industry, the crisis coming periodically nearly every ten years, and throwing out of employment several hundred thousand men who are brought to complete misery, whose children grow up in the gutter, ready to become inmates of the prison and workhouse. The workmen being unable to purchase with their wages the riches they are producing, industry must search for markets elsewhere, amidst the middle classes of other nations. It must find markets, in the East, in Africa, anywhere; it must increase, by trade, the number of its serfs in Egypt, in India, on the Congo. But everywhere it finds competitors in other nations which rapidly enter into the same line of industrial development. And wars, continuous wars, must be fought for the supremacy in the world-market — wars for the possession of the East, wars for getting possession of the seas, wars for the right of imposing heavy duties on foreign merchandise. The thunder of European guns never ceases; whole generations are slaughtered from time to time; and we spend in armaments the third of the revenue of our States — a revenue raised, the poor know with what difficulties.

Education is the privilege of the few. Not because we can find no teachers, not because the workman's son and daughter are less able to receive instruction, but because one can receive no reasonable instruction when at the age of fifteen he descends into the mine, or goes selling newspapers in the streets. Society becomes divided into two hostile camps; and no freedom is possible under such conditions. While the Radical asks for a further extension of liberty, the statesman answers him that a further increase of liberty would bring about an uprising of the paupers; and those political liberties which have cost so dear are replaced by coercion, by exceptional laws, by military rule.

And finally, the injustice of our partition of wealth exercises the most deplorable effect on our morality. Our principles of morality say: 'Love your neighbour as yourself'; but let a child follow this principle and take off his coat to give it to the shivering pauper, and his mother will tell him that he must never understand moral principles in their direct sense. If he lives according to them, he will go barefoot, without alleviating the misery round about him! Morality is good on the lips, not in deeds. Our preachers say, 'Who works, prays', and everybody endeavours to make others work for him. They say, 'Never lie!', and politics are a big lie. And we accustom ourselves and our children to live under this double-faced morality, which is hypocrisy, and to conciliate our double-facedness by sophistry. Hypocrisy and sophistry become the very basis of our life. But society cannot live under such a morality. It cannot last so: it must, it will, be changed.

The question is thus no more a mere question of bread. It covers the whole field of human activity. But it has at its bottom a question of social economy, and we conclude: The means of production and of satisfaction of all needs of society, having been created by the common efforts of all, must be at the disposal of all. The private appropriation of requisites for production is neither just nor beneficial. All must be placed on the same footing as producers and consumers of wealth. That will be the only way for society to step out of the bad conditions which have been created by centuries of wars and oppression. That will be the only guarantee for further progress in a direction of equality and freedom, which have always been the real, although unspoken goal of humanity.

II

The views taken in the above as to the combination of efforts being the chief source of our wealth explain why most Anarchists see in Communism the only equitable solution as to the adequate remuneration of individual efforts. There was a time when a family engaged in agriculture supplemented by a few domestic trades, could consider the corn they raised and the plain woollen cloth they wove as productions of their own and nobody else's labour. Even then such a view was not quite correct: there were forests cleared and roads built by common efforts; and even then the family had continually to apply for communal help, as is still the case in so many village communities. But now, in the extremely interwoven state of industry of which each branch supports all others, such an individualistic view can be held no more. If the iron trade and the cotton industry of this country have reached so high a degree of development, they have done so owing to the parallel growth of thousands of other industries, great and small; to the extension of the railway system; to an increase of knowledge among both the skilled engineers and the mass of the workmen; to a certain training in organisation slowly developed among British producers; and, above all, to the world-trade which has itself grown up, thanks to works executed thousands of miles away. The Italians who died from cholera in digging the Suez Canal, or from 'tunnel-disease' in the St Gotthard Tunnel, have contributed as much towards the enrichment of this country as the British girl who is prematurely growing old in serving a machine at Manchester; and this girl as much as the engineer who made a labour-saving improvement in our machinery. How can we pretend to estimate the exact part of each of them in the riches accumulated around us?

We may admire the inventive genius or the organising capacities of an iron lord; but we must recognise that all his genius and energy would not realise one-tenth of what they realise here if they were spent in dealing with Mongolian shepherds or Siberian peasants instead of British workmen, British engineers, and trustworthy managers. An English millionaire who succeeded in giving a powerful impulse to a branch of home industry was asked the other day what were, in his opinion, the real causes of his success. His answer was: 'I always sought out the right man for a given branch of the concern, and I left him full independence — maintaining, of course, for myself the general supervision.' 'Did you never fail to find such men?' was the next question. 'Never.' 'But in the new branches which you introduced you wanted a number of new inventions.' 'No doubt; we spent thousands in buying patents.' This little colloquy sums up, in my opinion, the real case of those industrial undertakings which are quoted by the advocates of 'an adequate remuneration of individual efforts' in the shape of millions bestowed on the managers of prosperous industries. It shows in how far the efforts are really 'individual'. Leaving aside the thousand conditions which sometimes permit a man to show, and sometimes prevent him from showing, his capacities to their full extent, it might be asked in how far the same capacities could bring out the same results, if the very same employer could find no trustworthy managers and no skilled workmen, and if hundreds of inventions were not stimulated by the mechanical turn of mind of so many inhabitants of this country. British industry is the work of the British nation — nay, of Europe and India taken together — not of separate individuals.

While holding this synthetic view on production, the Anarchists cannot consider, like the Collectivists, that a remuneration which would be proportionate to the hours of labour spent by each person in the production of riches may be an ideal, or even an approach to an ideal, society. Without entering here into a discussion as to how far the exchange value of each merchandise is really measured now by the amount of labour necessary for its production — a separate study must be devoted to the subject — we must say that the Collectivist ideal seems to us merely unrealisable in a society which has been brought to consider the necessaries for production as a common property. Such a society would be compelled to abandon the wage system altogether. It appears impossible that the mitigated Individualism of the Collectivist school could coexist with the partial Communism implied by holding land and machinery in common — unless imposed by a powerful government, much more powerful than all those of our own times. The present wage system has grown up from the appropriation of the necessaries for production by the few; it was a necessary condition for the growth of the present capitalist production; and it cannot outlive it, even if an attempt be made to pay to the worker the full value of his produce, and hours-of-labour cheques be substituted for money. Common possession of the necessaries for production implies the common enjoyment of the fruits of the common production; and we consider that an equitable organisation of society can only arise when every wage system is abandoned, and when everybody, contributing for the common well-being to the full extent of his capacities, shall enjoy also from the common stock of society to the fullest possible extent of his needs.

We maintain, moreover, not only that Communism is a desirable state of society, but that the growing tendency of modern society is precisely towards Communism — free Communism — notwithstanding the seemingly contradictory growth of Individualism. In the growth of Individualism (especially during the last three centuries) we merely see the endeavours of the individual towards emancipating himself from the steadily growing powers of Capital and the State. But side by side with this growth we see also, throughout history up to our own times, the latent struggle of the producers of wealth to maintain the partial Communism of old, as well as to reintroduce Communist principles in a new shape, as soon as favourable conditions permit it. As soon as the communes of the tenth, eleventh and twelfth centuries were enabled to start their own independent life, they gave a wide extension to work in common, to trade in common, and to a partial consumption in common. All this has disappeared; but the rural commune fights a hard struggle to maintain its old features, and it succeeds in maintaining them in many places of Eastern Europe, Switzerland, and even France and Germany; while new organisations, based on the same principles, never fail to grow up wherever it is possible. Notwithstanding the egotistic turn given to the public mind by the merchant-production of our century, the Communist tendency is continually reasserting itself and trying to make its way into public life. The penny bridge disappears before the public bridge; and the turnpike road before the free road. The same spirit pervades thousands of other institutions. Museums, free libraries, and free public schools; parks and pleasure grounds; paved and lighted streets, free for everybody's use; water supplied to private dwellings, with a growing tendency towards disregarding the exact amount of it used by the individual; tramways and railways which have already begun to introduce the season ticket or the uniform tax, and will surely go much further on this line when they are no longer private property: all these are tokens showing in what direction further progress is to be expected.

It is in the direction of putting the wants of the individual *above* the valuation of the services he has rendered, or might render, to society; in considering society as a whole, so intimately connected together that a service rendered to any individual is a service rendered to the whole society. The librarian of the British Museum does not ask the reader what have been his previous services to society, he simply gives him the books he requires; and for a uniform fee, a scientific Society leaves its gardens and museums at the free disposal of each member. The crew of a lifeboat do not ask whether the men of a distressed ship are entitled to be rescued at a risk of life; and the Prisoners' Aid Society do not inquire what a released prisoner is worth. Here are men in need of a service; they are *fellow* men, and no further rights are required. And if this very city, so egotistic today, be visited by a public calamity — let it be besieged, for example, like Paris in 1871, and experience during the siege a want of food — this very same city would be unanimous in proclaiming that the first needs to be satisfied are those of the children and old, no matter what services they may render or have rendered to society. And it would take care of the active defenders of the city, whatever the degrees of gallantry displayed by each of them. But, this tendency already existing, nobody will deny, I suppose, that, in proportion as humanity is relieved from its hard struggle for life, the same tendency will grow stronger. If our productive powers were fully applied to increasing the stock of the staple necessities for life; if a modification of the present conditions of property increased the number of producers by all those who are not producers of wealth now; and if manual labour reconquered its place of honour in society — all this decuplating our production and rendering labour easier and more attractive — the Communist tendencies already existing would immediately enlarge their sphere of application.

Taking all this into account, and still more the practical aspects of the question as to how private property *might* become common property, most of the Anarchists maintain that the very next step to be made by society, as soon as the present regime of property undergoes a modification, will be in a Communist sense. We are Communists. But our Communism is not that of either the Phalanstery or the authoritarian school: it is Anarchist Communism, Communism without government, free Communism. It is a synthesis of the two chief aims prosecuted by humanity since the dawn of its history — economical freedom and political freedom.

I have already said that anarchy means no-government. We know well that the word 'anarchy' is also used in current phraseology as synonymous with disorder. But that meaning of 'anarchy' being a derived one, implies at least two suppositions. It implies, first, that wherever there is no government there is disorder; and it implies, moreover, that order, due to a strong government and a strong police, is always beneficial. Both implications, however, are anything but proved. There is plenty of order — we should say, of harmony — in many branches of human activity where the government, happily, does not interfere. As to the beneficial effects of order, the kind of order that reigned at Naples under the Bourbons surely was not preferable to some disorder started by Garibaldi; while the Protestants of this country will probably say that the good deal of disorder made by Luther was preferable, at any rate, to the order which reigned under the Pope. As to the proverbial 'order' which was once 'restored at Warsaw', there are, I suppose, no two opinions about it. While all agree that harmony is always desirable, there is no such unanimity about order, and still less about the 'order' which is supposed to reign in our modern societies; so that we have no objection whatever to the use of the word 'anarchy' as a negation of what has often been described as order.

By taking for our watchword anarchy, in its sense of no-government, we intend to express a pronounced tendency of human society. In history we see that precisely those epochs when small parts of humanity broke down the power of their rulers and reassumed their freedom were epochs of the greatest progress, economical and intellectual. Be it the growth of the free cities, whose unrivalled monuments — free work of free associations of workers — still testify of the revival of mind and of the well-being of the citizen; be it the great movement which gave birth to the Reformation — those epochs when the individual recovered some part of his freedom witnessed the greatest progress. And if we carefully watch the present development of civilised nations, we cannot fail to discover in it a marked and ever-growing movement towards limiting more and more the sphere of action of government, so as to leave more and more liberty to the initiative of the individual. After having tried all kinds of government, and endeavoured to solve the insoluble problem of having a government 'which might compel the individual to obedience, without escaping itself from obedience to collectivity', humanity is trying now to free itself from the bonds of any government whatever, and to respond to its needs of organisation by the free understanding between individuals prosecuting the same common aims. Home Rule, even for the smallest territorial unit or group, becomes a growing need; free agreement is becoming a substitute for law; and free cooperation a substitute for governmental guardianship. One after the other those functions which were considered as the functions of government during the last two centuries, are disputed; society moves better the less it is governed. And the more we study the advance made in this direction, as well as the inadequacy of governments to fulfil the expectations placed in them, the more we are bound to conclude that Humanity, by steadily limiting the functions of government, is marching towards reducing them finally to nil; and we already foresee a state of society where the liberty of the individual will be limited by no laws, no bonds — by nothing else but his own social habits and the necessity, which everyone feels, of finding cooperation, support, and sympathy among his neighbours.

Of course, the no-government ethics will meet with at least as many objections as the no-capital economics. Our minds have been so nurtured in prejudices as to the providential functions of government that Anarchist ideas *must* be received with distrust. Our whole education from childhood to the grave, nurtures the belief in the necessity of a government and its beneficial effects. Systems of philosophy have been elaborated to support this view; history has been written from this standpoint; theories of law have been circulated and taught for the same purpose. All politics are based on the same principle, each politician saying to people he wants to support him: 'Give me the governmental power; I will, I can, relieve you from the hardships of your present life.' All our education is permeated with the same teachings. We may open any book of sociology, history, law, or ethics: everywhere we find government, its organisation, its deeds, playing so prominent a part that we grow accustomed to suppose that the State and the political men are everything; that there is nothing behind the big statesmen. The same teachings are daily repeated in the Press. Whole columns are filled up with minutest records of parliamentary debates, of movements of political persons; and, while reading these columns, we too often forget that there is an immense body of men — mankind, in fact — growing and dying, living in happiness or sorrow, labouring and consuming, thinking and creating, besides those few men whose importance has been so swollen up as to overshadow humanity.

And yet, if we revert from the printed matter to our real life, and cast a broad glance on society as it is, we are struck with the infinitesimal part played by government in our life. Millions of human beings live and die without having had anything to do with government. Every day millions of transactions are made without the slightest interference of government; and those who enter into agreements have not the slightest intention of breaking bargains. Nay, those agreements which are not protected by government (those of the Exchange, or card debts) are perhaps better kept than any others. The simple habit of keeping one's word, the desire of not losing confidence, are quite sufficient in an overwhelming majority of cases to enforce the keeping of agreements. Of course, it may be said that there is still the government which might enforce them if necessary. But not to speak of the numberless cases which could not even be brought before a court, everybody who has the slightest acquaintance with trade will undoubtedly confirm the assertion that, if there were not so strong a feeling of honour in keeping agreements, trade itself would become utterly impossible.

Even those merchants and manufacturers who feel not the slightest remorse when poisoning their customers with all kinds of abominable drugs, duly labelled, even they also keep their commercial agreements. But if such a relative morality as commercial honesty exists now, under the present conditions, when enrichment is the chief motive, the same feeling will further develop very fast as soon as robbing somebody of the fruits of his labour is no longer the economical basis of our life.

Another striking feature of our century tells in favour of the same no-government tendency. It is the steady enlargement of the field covered by private initiative, and the recent growth of large organisations resulting merely and simply from free agreement. The railway net of Europe — a confederation of so many scores of separate societies — and the direct transport of passengers and merchandise over so many lines which were built independently and federated together, without even so much as a Central Board of European Railways, are a most striking instance of what is already done by mere agreement. If fifty years ago somebody had predicted that railways built by so many separate companies finally would constitute so perfect a net as they do today, he surely would have been treated as a fool. It would have been urged that so many companies, prosecuting their own interests, would never agree without an International Board of Railways, supported by an International Convention of the European States, and endowed with governmental powers. But no such board was resorted to, and the agreement came nevertheless. The Dutch *Beurden*, or associations of ship and boat owners, are extending now their organisations over the rivers of Germany, and even to the shipping trade of the Baltic; the numberless amalgamated manufacturers' associations, and the *Syndicats* of France, are so many instances in point. If it be argued that many of these organisations are organisations for exploitation, that proves nothing, because, if men prosecuting their own egotistic, often very narrow, interests can agree together, better-inspired men, compelled to be more closely connected with other groups, will necessarily agree still more easily and still better.

But there also is no lack of free organisations for nobler pursuits. One of the noblest achievements of our century is undoubtedly the

Lifeboat Association. Since its first humble start, which we all remember, it has saved no less than 32,000 human lives. It makes appeal to the noblest instincts of man; its activity is entirely dependent upon devotion to the common cause; while its internal organisation is entirely based upon the independence of the local committees. The Hospitals Association and hundreds of like organisations, operating on a large scale and covering each a wide field, may also be mentioned under this head. But, while we know everything about governments and their deeds, what do we know about the results achieved by free cooperation? Thousands of volumes have been written to record the acts of governments; the most trifling amelioration due to law has been recorded; its good effects have been exaggerated, its bad effects passed by in silence. But where is the book recording what has been achieved by free cooperation of well-inspired men? — At the same time, hundreds of societies are constituted every day for the satisfaction of some of the infinitely varied needs of civilised man. We have societies for all possible kinds of studies — some of them embracing the whole field of natural science, others limited to a small special branch; societies for gymnastics, for shorthand-writing, for the study of a separate author, for games and all kinds of sports, for forwarding the science of maintaining life, and for favouring the art of destroying it; philosophical and industrial, artistic and anti-artistic; for serious work and for mere amusement — in short, there is not a single direction in which men exercise their faculties without combining together for the prosecution of some common aim. Every day new societies are formed, while every year the old ones aggregate together into larger units, federate across the national frontiers, and cooperate in some common work.

The most striking feature of these numberless free growths is that they continually encroach on what was formerly the domain of the State or the Municipality. A householder in a Swiss village on the banks of Lake Leman belongs now to, at least, a dozen different societies which supply him with what is considered elsewhere as a function of the municipal government. Free federation of independent communes for temporary or permanent purposes lies at the very bottom of Swiss life, and to these federations many a part of Switzerland is indebted for its roads and fountains, its rich vineyards, well-kept forests, and meadows which the foreigner admires. And besides these small societies, substituting themselves for the State within some limited sphere, do we not see other societies doing the same on a much wider scale? Each German *Burger* is proud of the German army, but few of them know how much of its strength is borrowed from the numberless private societies for military studies, exercises, and games; and how few are those who understand that their army would become an incoherent mass of men on the day when each soldier was no longer inspired by the feelings which inspire him now? In this country, even the task of defending the territory — that is, the chief, the great function of the State — has been undertaken by an army of Volunteers, and this army surely might stand against any army of slaves obeying a military despot. More than that: a private society for the defence of the coasts of England has been seriously spoken of. Let it only come into life, and surely it will be a more effective weapon for self-defence than the ironclads of the navy. One of the most remarkable societies, however, which has recently arisen is undoubtedly the Red Cross Society. To slaughter men on the battle-fields, that remains the duty of the State; but these very States recognise their inability to take care of their own wounded: they abandon the task, to a great extent, to private initiative. What a deluge of mockeries would not have been cast over the poor 'Utopist' who should have dared to say twenty-five years ago that the care of the wounded might be left to private societies! 'Nobody would go into the dangerous places! Hospitals would all gather where there was no need of them! National rivalries would result in the poor soldiers dying without any help, and so on.' — Such would have been the outcry. The war of 1871 has shown how perspicacious those prophets are who never believe in human intelligence, devotion, and good sense.

These facts — so numerous and so customary that we pass by without even noticing them — are in our opinion one of the most prominent features of the second half of our century. The just-mentioned organisms grew up so naturally; they so rapidly extended and so easily aggregated together; they are such unavoidable out-growths of the multiplication of needs of the civilised man, and they so well replace State-interference, that we must recognise in them a growing factor of our life. Modern progress is really towards the free aggregation of free individuals so as to supplant government in all those functions which formerly were entrusted to it, and which it mostly performed so badly.

As to parliamentary rule, and representative government altogether, they are rapidly falling into decay. The few philosophers who already have shown their defects have only timidly summed up the growing public discontent. It is becoming evident that it is merely stupid to elect a few men, and to entrust them with the task of making laws on all possible subjects, of which subjects most of them are utterly ignorant. It is becoming understood that Majority rule is as defective as any other kind of rule; and Humanity searches, and finds, new channels for resolving the pending questions. The Postal Union did not elect an international postal parliament in order to make laws for all postal organisations adherent to the Union. The railways of Europe did not elect an international railway parliament in order to regulate the running of the trains and the partition of the income of international traffic; and the Meteorological and Geological Societies of Europe did not elect either meteorological or geological parliaments to plan polar stations, or to establish a uniform subdivision of geological formations and a uniform coloration of geological maps. They proceeded by means of agreement. To agree together they resorted to congresses; but while sending delegates to their congresses, they did not elect MPs *bons à tout faire*; they did not say to them, 'Vote about everything you like — we shall obey.' They put questions and discussed them first themselves; then they sent delegates acquainted with the special question to be discussed at the congress, and they sent *delegates* — not rulers. Their delegates returned from the congress with no *laws* in their pockets, but with *proposals of agreements*. Such is the way assumed now (the very old way, too) for dealing with questions of public interest — not the way of law-making by means of a representative government. Representative government has accomplished its historical mission; it has given a mortal blow to Court-rule; and by its debates it has awakened public interest in public questions. But, to see in it the government of the future Socialist society, is to commit a gross error. Each economical phase of life implies its own political phase;

and it is impossible to touch the very basis of the present economical life — private property — without a corresponding change in the very basis of the political organisation. Life already shows in which direction the change will be made. Not in increasing the powers of the State, but in resorting to free organisation and free federation in all those branches which are now considered as attributes of the State.

The objections to the above may be easily foreseen. It will be said of course: 'But what is to be done with those who do not keep their agreements? What with those who are not inclined to work? What with those who would prefer breaking the written laws of society, or — on the Anarchist hypothesis — its unwritten customs? Anarchy may be good for a higher humanity, — not for the men of our own times.'

First of all, there are two kinds of agreements: there is the free one which is entered upon by free consent, as a free choice between different courses equally open to each of the agreeing parties; and there is the enforced agreement, imposed by one party upon the other, and accepted by the latter from sheer necessity; in fact, it is no agreement at all; it is a mere submission to necessity. Unhappily, the great bulk of what are now described as agreements belong to the latter category. When a workman sells his labour to an employer, and knows perfectly well that some part of the value of his produce will be unjustly taken by the employer; when he sells it without even the slightest guarantee of being employed so much as six consecutive months — and he is compelled to do so because he and his family would otherwise starve next week — it is a sad mockery to call that a free contract. Modern economists may call it free, but the father of political economy — Adam Smith — was never guilty of such a misrepresentation. As long as three-quarters of humanity are compelled to enter into agreements of that description, force is, of course, necessary, both to enforce the supposed agreements and to maintain such a state of things. Force — and a good deal of force — is necessary to prevent the labourers from taking possession of what they consider unjustly appropriated by the few; and force is necessary to continually bring new 'uncivilised nations' under the same conditions. The Spencerian no-force party perfectly well understand that; and while they advocate no force for changing the existing conditions, they advocate still more force than is now used for maintaining them. As to Anarchy, it is obviously as incompatible with plutocracy as with any other kind of -*cracy*.

But we do not see the necessity of force for enforcing agreements freely entered upon. We never heard of a penalty imposed on a man who belonged to the crew of a lifeboat and at a given moment preferred to abandon the association. All that his comrades would do with him, if he were guilty of a gross neglect, would be probably to refuse to do anything further with him. Nor did we hear of fines imposed on a contributor to Mr Murray's Dictionary for a delay in his work, or of gendarmes driving the volunteers of Garibaldi to the battlefield. Free agreements need not be enforced.

As to the so-often repeated objection that nobody would labour if he were not compelled to do so by sheer necessity, we heard enough of it before the emancipation of slaves in America, as well as before the emancipation of serfs in Russia; and we have had the opportunity of appreciating it at its just value. So we shall not try to convince those who can be convinced only by accomplished facts. As to those who reason, they ought to know that, if it really was so with some parts of humanity at its lowest stages — and yet, what do we know about it? — or if it is so with some small communities, or separate individuals, brought to sheer despair by ill success in their struggle against unfavourable conditions, it is not so with the bulk of the civilised nations. With us, work is a habit, and idleness an artificial growth. Of course, when to be a manual worker means to be compelled to work all one's life long for ten hours a day, and often more, at producing some part of something — a pin's head, for instance; when it means to be paid wages on which a family can live only on the condition of the strictest limitation of all its needs; when it means to be always under the menace of being thrown tomorrow out of employment — and we know how frequent are the industrial crises, and what misery they imply; when it means, in a very great number of cases, premature death in a paupers' infirmary, if not in the workhouse; when to be a manual worker signifies to wear a lifelong stamp of inferiority in the eyes of those very people who live on the work of their 'hands'; when it always means the renunciation of all those higher enjoyments that science and art give to man — oh, then there is no wonder that everybody — the manual worker as well — has but one dream: that of rising to a condition where others would work for him. When I see writers who boast that they are the workers, and write that the manual workers are an inferior race of lazy and improvident fellows, I must ask them: Who, then, has made all you see round about you: the houses you live in, the chairs, the carpets, the streets you enjoy, the clothes you wear? Who built the universities where you were taught, and who provided you with food during your school years? And what would become of your readiness to 'work', if you were compelled to work in the above conditions all your life at a pin's head? No doubt, anyhow *you* would be reported as a lazy fellow! And I affirm that no intelligent man can be closely acquainted with the life of the European working classes without wondering, on the contrary, at their readiness to work, even under such abominable conditions.

Overwork is repulsive to human nature — not work. Overwork for supplying the few with luxury — not work for the well-being of all. Work, labour, is a physiological necessity, a necessity of spending accumulated bodily energy, a necessity which is health and life itself. If so many branches of useful work are so reluctantly done now, it is merely because they mean overwork, or they are improperly organised. But we know — old Franklin knew it — that four hours of useful work every day would be more than sufficient for supplying everybody with the comfort of a moderately well-to-do middle-class house, if we all gave ourselves to productive work, and if we did not waste our productive powers as we do waste them now. As to the childish question, repeated for fifty years, 'Who would do disagreeable work?', frankly I regret that none of our savants has ever been brought to do it, be it for only one day in his life. If there is still work which is really disagreeable in itself, it is only because our scientific men have never cared to consider the means of rendering it less so: they have always known that there were plenty of starving men who would do it for a few pence a day.

As to the third — the chief — objection, which maintains the necessity of a government for punishing those who break the law of society, there is so much to say about it that it hardly can be touched incidentally.[5] The more we study the question, the more we are brought to the conclusion that society itself is responsible for the anti-social deeds perpetrated in its midst, and that no punishment, no prisons, and no hangmen can diminish the numbers of such deeds; nothing short of a reorganisation of society itself. Three-quarters of all the acts which are brought every year before our courts have their origin, either directly or indirectly, in the present disorganised state of society with regard to the production and distribution of wealth — not in the perversity of human nature. As to the relatively few anti-social deeds which result from anti-social inclinations of separate individuals, it is not by prisons, nor even by resorting to the hangmen, that we can diminish their numbers. By our prisons, we merely multiply them and render them worse. By our detectives, our 'price of blood', our executions, and our jails, we spread in society such a terrible flow of basest passions and habits, that he who should realise the effects of these institutions to their full extent, would be frightened by what society is doing under the pretext of maintaining morality. We *must* search for other remedies, and the remedies have been indicated long since.

Of course now, when a mother in search of food and shelter for her children must pass by shops filled with the most refined delicacies of refined gluttony; when gorgeous and insolent luxury is displayed side by side with the most execrable misery; when the dog and the horse of a rich man are far better cared for than millions of children whose mothers earn a pitiful salary in the pit or the manufactory; when each 'modest' evening dress of a lady represents eight months, or one year, of human labour; when enrichment at somebody else's expense is the avowed aim of the 'upper classes', and no distinct boundary can be traced between honest and dishonest means of making money — then force is the only means for maintaining such a state of things; then an army of policemen, judges, and hangmen becomes a necessary institution.

But if all our children — all children are *our* children — received

---

5 Some more upon this subject is said in the last two chapters of *In Russian and French Prisons*.

a sound instruction and education — and we have the means of giving it; if every family lived in a decent home — and they *could* at the present high pitch of our production; if every boy and girl were taught a handicraft at the same time as he or she receives scientific instruction, and *not* to be a manual producer of wealth were considered as a token of inferiority; if men lived in closer contact with one another, and had continually to come into contact on those public affairs which now are vested in the few; and if, in consequence of a closer contact, we were brought to take as lively an interest in our neighbours' difficulties and pains as we formerly took in those of our kinsfolk — then we should not resort to policemen and judges, to prisons and executions. Anti-social deeds would be nipped in the bud, not punished; the few contests which would arise would be easily settled by arbitrators; and no more force would be necessary to impose their decisions than is required now for enforcing the decisions of the family tribunals of China, or of the Valencia water-courts.

And here we are brought to consider a great question: what would become of morality in a society which recognised no laws and proclaimed the full freedom of the individual? Our answer is plain. Public morality is independent from, and anterior to, law and religion. Until now, the teachings of morality have been associated with religious teachings. But the influence which religious teachings formerly exercised on the mind has faded of late, and the sanction which morality derived from religion has no longer the power it formerly had. Millions and millions grow in our cities who have lost the old faith. Is it a reason for throwing morality overboard, and for treating it with the same sarcasm as primitive cosmogony?

Obviously not. No society is possible without certain principles of morality generally recognised. If everybody grew accustomed to deceive his fellow-men; if we never could rely on each other's promise and words; if everybody treated his fellow as an enemy, against whom every means of warfare is justifiable — no society could exist. And we see, in fact, that notwithstanding the decay of religious beliefs, the principles of morality remain unshaken. We even see irreligious people trying to raise the current standard of morality. The fact is that moral principles are independent of religious beliefs: they are anterior to them. The primitive Tchuktchis have no religion: they have only superstitions and fear of the hostile forces of nature; and nevertheless we find them with the very same principles of morality which are taught by Christians and Buddhists, Mussulmans and Hebrews. Nay, some of their practices imply a much higher standard of tribal morality than that which appears in our civilised society. In fact, each new religion takes its moral principles from the only real stock of morality — the moral habits which grow with men as soon as they unite to live together in tribes, cities, or nations. No animal society is possible without resulting in a growth of certain moral habits of mutual support and even self-sacrifice for the common well-being. These habits are a necessary condition for the welfare of the species in its struggle for life — cooperation of individuals being a much more important factor in the struggle for the preservation of the species than the so-much-spoken-of physical struggle between individuals for the means of existence. The 'fittest' in the organic world are those who grow accustomed to life in society; and life in society necessarily implies moral habits. As to mankind, it has, during its long existence, developed in its midst a nucleus of social habits, of moral habits, which cannot disappear as long as human societies exist. And therefore, notwithstanding the influences to the contrary which are now at work in consequence of our present economical relations, the nucleus of our moral habits continues to exist. Law and religion only formulate them and endeavour to enforce them by their sanction.

Whatever the variety of theories of morality, all can be brought under three chief categories: the morality of religion; the utilitarian morality; and the theory of moral habits resulting from the very needs of life in society. Each religious morality sanctifies its prescriptions by making them originate from revelation; and it tries to impress its teachings on the mind by a promise of reward, or punishment, either in this or in a future life. The utilitarian morality maintains the idea of reward, but it finds it in man himself. It invites men to analyse their pleasures, to classify them, and to give preference to those which are most intense and most durable. We must recognise, however, that, although it has exercised some influence, this system has been judged too artificial by the great mass of human beings. And finally — whatever its varieties — there is the third system of morality which sees in moral actions — in those actions which are most powerful in rendering men best fitted for life in society — a mere necessity of the individual to enjoy the joys of his brethren, to suffer when some of his brethren are suffering; a habit and a second nature, slowly elaborated and perfected by life in society. That is the morality of mankind; and that is also the morality of Anarchy.

I could not better illustrate the difference between the three systems of morality than by repeating the following example. Suppose a child is drowning in the river, and three men stand on the bank of the river: the religious moralist, the utilitarian, and the plain man of the people. The religious man is supposed, first, to say to himself that to save the child would bring him happiness in this or another life, and then save the child; but if he does so, he is merely a good reckoner, no more. Then comes the utilitarian, who is supposed to reason thus: 'The enjoyment of life may be of the higher and of the lower description. To save the child would assure me the higher enjoyment. Therefore, let me jump into the river.' But, admitting that there ever was a man who reasoned in this way, again, he would be a mere reckoner, and society would do better not to rely very much upon him: who knows what sophism might pass one day through his head! And here is the third man. He does not calculate much. But he has grown in the habit of always feeling the joys of those who surround him, and feeling happy when others are happy; of suffering, deeply suffering when others suffer. To act accordingly is his second nature. He hears the cry of the mother, he sees the child struggling for life, and he jumps into the river like a good dog, and saves the child, thanks to the energy of his feelings. And when the mother thanks him, he answers: 'Why! I could not do otherwise than I did.' That is the real morality. That is the morality of the masses of the people; the morality grown to a habit, which will exist, whatever the ethical theories made by philosophers, and will steadily improve in proportion as the conditions of our social life are improved. Such a morality needs no law for its maintenance. It is a natural growth favoured by the general sympathy which every advance towards a wider and higher morality finds in all fellow-men.

Such are, in a very brief summary, the leading principles of Anarchy. Each of them hurts many a prejudice, and yet each of them results from an analysis of the very tendencies displayed by human society. Each of them is rich in consequences and implies a thorough revision of many a current opinion. And Anarchy is not a mere insight into a remote future. Already now, whatever the sphere of action of the individual, he can act, either in accordance with Anarchist principles or on an opposite line. And all that may be done in that direction will be done in the direction whereto further development goes. All that may be done in the opposite way will be an attempt to force humanity to go where it will *not* go.

Bibliography

Anarchist Communism was first published as a pair of articles in *The Nineteenth Century* (edited by James Knowles) — 'The Scientific Bases of Anarchy' (120, February 1887), and 'The Coming Anarchy' (126, August 1887) — both signed 'P. Kropotkin'. The long interval between the articles was explained in an editorial footnote to the second: 'The present article has been delayed in consequence of the illness of the author'. (Other reasons may have been the illness of his wife and the birth of their daughter.)

The articles were not at first reprinted in Britain, because of copyright difficulties, although an extract was published in Henry Seymour's paper *The Anarchist* (April 1887). But they were quickly reprinted in the United States — first in *The Eclectic Magazine of Foreign Literature, Science and Art* (April and October 1887), a New York monthly which reprinted articles from the British press, and then in *Anarchism: Its Philosophy and Scientific Basis*, a book which was edited by Albert Parsons, the only native American among the Haymarket Martyrs, during his imprisonment in 1886-1887, and published in Chicago (in both English and German) by his wife Lucy Parsons immediately after his execution in November 1887; it contained a miscellaneous collection of material on and by the Haymarket Martyrs and also some more general items by well-known socialists, including Karl Marx (!) as well as Reclus and Kropotkin.

The pair of articles was eventually reprinted in Britain in 1891 as the fourth Freedom Pamphlet,'republished by permission of the Editor from the *Nineteenth Century*' and 'revised by the Author', with the title *Anarchist Communism: Its Basis and Principles*, signed 'Peter Kropotkine'. This edition was frequently reprinted by the Freedom Press during the next thirty years (1895, 1897, 1900, 1905, 1913, 1920). It was serialised in the American *Freedom* during 1892; it was later serialised in the rival British *Freedom* during 1932-1933, and then reprinted as a pair of pamphlets, the fourth and fifth Freedom Publications, edited by George Cores. It was translated into several other languages.

The pamphlet version has frequently been included in collections of Kropotkin's writings or anthologies of anarchist writings, generally in an inaccurate or incomplete form. This is the first complete edition for more than half a century. The text follows the version of 1891, with the minimum of alteration to correct misprints and to regularise spelling, capitalisation and punctuation.

Notes

No attempt has been made to explain all Kropotkin's many references, most of which may easily be traced in standard reference books, but a few points have been explored.

Page 24 *Utopists*. The early nineteenth-century socialists who concentrated on the theoretical principles of future society rather than the practical problems of achieving it — especially Robert Owen, Henri de Saint-Simon, Auguste Comte, and Charles Fourier.

Page 27 *Caesarism*. The usurpation of power by a popular leader who then establishes a personal dictatorship — as by Julius Caesar and then by his great-nephew Augustus in ancient Rome, or by Napoléon Bonaparte and then by his nephew Louis Napoléon in modern France, or by Communist and Fascist rulers during the twentieth century.

Page 27 *Volksstaat* and *Kulturstaat*. German conceptions of the State. *Volksstaat* (People's State) was a conception of Marxists (though not of Marx himself) in which an all-powerful State represents the whole people. *Kulturstaat* (Cultural State) was a conception of Idealist philosophers (especially Hegel) in which an all-powerful State represents the whole nation.

Page 28 *Communes*. The Commune movement which swept France and Spain in 1870-1873 was a central element in Kropotkin's theory of anarchist communism.

Pages 30-31 *Herbert Spencer*. The leading British liberal thinker of the late nineteenth century founded what he called the Synthetic Philosophy, attempting to combine natural and social science and to develop a single evolutionary theory for all living systems, human society being seen by analogy as an organic growth. His political theory of extreme liberalism anticipated what is now called Libertarianism. Kropotkin acknowledged his significance in many writings, but opposed his scientific and political dogmatism.

Spencer's *Essays: Scientific, Political, and Speculative* appeared in three volumes from 1857 to 1874 (and in a revised edition in 1891); Kropotkin's references are to the 1874 volume. The quotation in the text comes from 'Reasons for Dissenting from Comte', the appendix to *The Classification of the Sciences* (first published as a pamphlet in 1864). Opposing Comte's advocacy of a strong government by an intellectual élite, Spencer argued: 'That form of society towards which we are progressing, I hold to be one in which *government* will be reduced to the smallest amount possible, and *freedom* increased to the greatest amount possible — one in which human nature will have become so moulded by social discipline into fitness for the social state, that it will need little external restraint, but will be self-restrained — one in which the citizen will tolerate no interference with his freedom, save that which maintains the equal freedom of others — one in which the spontaneous cooperation which has developed our industrial system, and is now developing with increasing rapidity, will produce agencies for the discharge of nearly all social functions, and will leave to the primary governmental agency nothing beyond the function of maintaining those conditions to free action, which make such spontaneous cooperation possible — one in which individual life will thus be pushed to the greatest extent consistent with social life; and in which social life will have no other end than to maintain the completest sphere for individual life.' The quotation in the footnote comes from 'Specialised Administration' (first published in *The Fortnightly Review* in December 1871). Opposing Proudhon's advocacy of anarchy, Spencer argued: 'I hold that within its proper limits governmental action is not simply legitimate but all-important....Not only do I contend that the restraining power of the State over individuals, and bodies or classes of individuals, is requisite, but I have contended that it should be exercised much more effectually, and carried out much further, than at present.' And he referred to the chapter on 'The Duty of the State' in his first book *Social Statics* (1851) — though not to the chapter on 'The Right to Ignore the State', which was omitted from later editions of the book and was published in several languages as an anarchist pamphlet!

Spencer's *The Data of Ethics*, the first part of *The Principles of Ethics*, was first published in 1879 (the other five parts following in 1891-1893). The appendix, which was added to the third edition in 1881, consists of a chapter called 'The Conciliation', which attempts to reconcile egoism and altruism in much the same way as Darwin and Kropotkin.

Page 33 (line 23) - **page 35** (line 12) This passage was reprinted in Henry Seymour's paper *The Anarchist* as an article with the title 'Kropotkine on Malthus's Fallacy' (April 1887). Kropotkin's critique of the doctrine of Thomas Malthus, in his *Essay on the Principle of Population* (1798, 1803), about the inevitable pressure of increasing population on available resources, follows the same line as William Godwin, and has turned out to be correct.

Page 34 *Khedive*. Title of Turkish viceroy of Egypt from 1867 to 1914, a byword for luxury and corruption.

Page 41 The *Suez Canal* in Egypt was built from 1859 to 1869; the British

NOTES 63

Government controlled the Suez Canal Company from 1875 to 1956. The *St Gotthard Tunnel* in Switzerland was built from 1872 to 1880.

Page 44 *The British Museum Library* (now called the British Library), which is the largest library in the country, allows free acess without qualification and with the minimum of formality.

Page 45 *Phalanstery.* The basic unit of Fourier's socialist Utopia, a highly structured large-scale commune.

Page 45 *Examples of undesirable order and desirable disorder.* Southern Italy was ruled by foreign dynasties from the Middle Ages, the last being the Bourbons, whose autocratic regime was based in Naples from the 1730s until it collapsed before Garibaldi's invasion of 1860, which led to the unification of Italy under a constitutional monarchy. The Roman Catholic regime in North-Western Europe was destroyed by the Protestant Reformation during the sixteenth century, started by Martin Luther. When Mikhail Muraviov, the Russian Governor of Poland, suppressed the nationalist uprising of 1863, he announced: 'Order has been restored in Warsaw.'

Page 47 *Free agreements.* Contracts made in commercial Exchanges and debts incurred in gambling have generally not been enforceable under English law.

Pages 48-51 *Examples of voluntary organisations.* The Royal National Lifeboat Institution, which was founded in 1824 to coordinate various organisations all over the country, began as and still remains a private organisation, independently administered and financed by voluntary donations. The many voluntary hospital associations were eventually largely absorbed by the National Health Service after 1947. The International Red Cross, which was formed in 1863 on the initiative of the Swiss reformer Henri Dunant, began as and still remains a private organisation, independently administered and financed by voluntary donations. The International Postal Union, which was formed in 1875, still coordinates national postal services on a federal basis. Later examples are the international agreements on air traffic and broadcasting.

Page 53 *Mr Murray's Dictionary.* James Murray edited *A New Dictionary on Historical Principles* from 1879 until his death in 1915; it was published by the Oxford University Press, supplementary volumes appearing until 1986, and is generally known as the *Oxford English Dictionary.* Most of its material has always been contributed by unpaid volunteers.

Page 54 *Benjamin Franklin* The leading American liberal thinker of the late eighteenth century in 1784 sent to his friend and editor Benjamin Vaughan, the radical British politician, a letter which was published anonymously in the London magazine *The Repository* in August 1788 and was reprinted in various editions of Franklin's works from 1793 onwards as an essay 'On Luxury, Idleness, and

Industry'. It includes the following passage: 'It has been computed by some political arithmetician, that if every man and woman would work for four hours each day on something useful, that labour would produce sufficient to procure all the necessaries and comforts of life, want and misery would be banished out of the world, and the rest of the twenty-four hours might be leisure and pleasure. What occasions then so much want and misery? It is the employment of men and women in works, that produce neither the necessaries nor conveniences of life, who, with those who do nothing, consume necessaries raised by the laborious.'

William Godwin went further a few years later, in *An Enquiry Concerning Political Justice* (1793): 'Half an hour a day, seriously employed in manual labour by every member of the community, would sufficiently supply the whole with necessaries' (Book VIII, Chapter 6 — later Chapter 8).

Page 57 *The Chukchis*, a Mongoloid people living in the remotest coastal region of Siberia, hardly support Kropotkin's point, since their moral code included polygamy and euthanasia!